THE ANVIL
Rings

ERIC LYONS, M.MIN.

APOLOGETICS PRESS

Apologetics Press, Inc.

230 Landmark Drive

Montgomery, Alabama 36117-2752

© Copyright 2003

ISBN: 0-932859-49-6

Library of Congress Cataloging-in-Publication

Eric Lyons, 1975 -

The Anvil Rings: Answers to Alleged Bible Discrepancies / Eric Lyons

Includes bibliographic references and subject, Scripture, and name indices.

ISBN 0-932859-49-6

1. Apologetics and polemics. 2. Christian Theology. I. Title

213–dc21   2003101533

DEDICATION

To my wife and best friend. Jana,
I love you "to the moon and back."

THE ANVIL

Last eve I passed beside a blacksmith's door,
And heard the anvil ring the vesper chime;
Then looking, I saw upon the floor,
Old hammers, worn with beating years of time.
"How many anvils have you had," said I,
"To wear and batter all these hammers so?"
"Just one," said he, and then with twinkling eye;
"The anvil wears the hammers out, ye know."
And so, thought I, the anvil of God's Word,
For ages skeptic blows have beat upon;
Yet though the noise of falling blows was heard
The anvil is unharmed...the hammers gone.

John Clifford (1836-1923)

TABLE OF CONTENTS

FOREWORD

His preacher described him as a "solid Christian." He was a young, dedicated follower of Christ who was enthusiastic about living for Jesus. From the time he was a young boy, his grandmother had taken him to worship God on the first day of every week. After becoming a Christian, he had, according to his preacher, "attended every service of the church." He grew in the faith, and began taking part in leading the congregation in prayer. Later, he personally taught the congregation by occasionally standing before the church and reading the Bible to them aloud, at times even delivering short talks. Before departing for the university an hour from his hometown, the young 18-year-old from West Virginia was considered by those who knew him best as a devout Christian with impressive potential—one whose shield of faith would stand strong when worldliness attacked, and whose Christian foundation would remain firm when shaken by the devil's doctrines.

Sadly, only a short time passed before this young man lost his faith. He went to college as a believer in the God of the Bible, and came home an "enlightened" skeptic. One of the first classes he took at the university was an elective course on world religions. Initially, he thought he could handle whatever questions came his way about Christianity. He had memorized nu-

merous verses in the Bible. He knew about the uniqueness of
the church. He could tell people what to do in order to have
their sins forgiven. It took, however, little time for **one** teacher
in **one** class in **one** university to turn this "solid Christian"
into an unbeliever.

What led to the demise of this young man's belief in God
and the Bible as His Word? Why did the young man's faith
crumble so easily? It all began with his inability to handle the
"factual discrepancies" that his newly found friends had convinced him were in the Bible. When asked to explain to his
teacher and fellow classmates how hundreds of "Bible contradictions" are not contradictions at all, but simply misun-
derstandings on man's part, he would not...because he could
not. After being bombarded with hundreds of questions that
he was incapable of answering, he eventually began denying
the truths he once believed. Not long after this young man's
"transformation," he gave one of his childhood mentors (the
preacher of the church where he was reared) a document titled "Factual Discrepancies." This document (of which I have
a copy) contains nearly seventy alleged "factual" contradictions that supposedly are found in the Bible. Because this frus-
trated young man from West Virginia (who had been taught
the Bible his entire life) was unable to answer these allegations,
he gave up on the God of the Bible. His faith in the inerrant,
inspired Word of God was replaced with the vacuousness of a
skeptic's uncertainty—all because he was unable to defend the
Truth against the vicious, frequent attacks leveled against it
by infidelity.

I wonder how many times this true story could be rehearsed
by mothers and fathers all over the world? How many grand-
mothers (like the one above) have seen their "work" (cf. 1 Corinthians 3:12-15) destroyed at the hands of infidels? How many
young college students leave home as "solid" Christians, and
return four years later as "enlightened" skeptics?

This reference book is dedicated to answering numerous alleged Bible contradictions, many of which were presented to the young West Virginian at the university he attended. It may be that you have never considered some of the questions this volume seeks to answer. Other questions, you will find, have been around for some time, but perhaps you have never heard them answered.

So far as ease of response is concerned, the questions and alleged discrepancies fall into various categories. Certain charges against God's Word are explained rather easily. Others require extensive research. It is a simple matter for the atheist, agnostic, or skeptic to charge that God's Word contains contradictions or discrepancies; it is not always a simple matter for the Bible believer to respond to such a claim. But, regardless of the ease or difficulty, it is my hope that you will see how the many "factual" discrepancies can be answered–logically and truthfully.

Eric Lyons
January 29, 2003

Chapter 1

ANSWERING THE ALLEGATIONS

THE NEED

Opponents of religion frequently have boasted of their ability to remove the Christian's foundation of faith by hacking away at the Bible. They believe that by chopping incessantly in the forest of inspiration with the cynical axe of criticism, they will be able to expunge the Bible from the masses, and push God from the Universe. Over 2,500 years ago, King Jehoiakim took his penknife, slashed the Old Testament Scriptures to pieces, and tossed them into a fire (Jeremiah 36:22-23). During the Middle Ages, attempts were made to keep the Bible from the man on the street. In fact, those caught translating or distributing the Scriptures often were subjected to imprisonment, torture, and even death. Centuries later, the French philosopher Voltaire (1694-1778) boastfully declared that there would not be a copy of the Bible on Earth within 100 years of his death. And in 1795, Thomas Paine arrogantly concluded in *The Age of Reason*:

> I have now gone through the Bible, as a man would
> go through a wood with an axe on his shoulder, and
> fell trees. Here they lie; and the priests, if they can,

may replant them. They may, perhaps, stick them
in the ground, but they will never make them grow
(p. 151).

The axe used by Paine, Voltaire, and others like them is most
often the alleged discrepancies or contradictions that they bra-
zenly brag can be demonstrated on practically every page and
in nearly every major premise of biblical teaching. Some years
ago, Dennis McKinsey, in his book, *The Encyclopedia of Biblical Errancy*, stated:

> Every analyst of the Bible should realize that the Book
> is a veritable miasma of contradictions, inconsisten-
> cies, inaccuracies, poor science, bad math, inaccurate
> geography, immoralities, degenerate heroes, false
> prophecies, boring repetitions, childish superstitions,
> silly miracles, and dry-as-dust discourse. **But con-
> tradictions remain the most obvious, the most
> potent, the most easily proven, and the most com-
> mon problem to plague the Book** (1995, p. 71, emp.
> added).

Steve Wells, author of the *Skeptic's Annotated Bible*, has claimed
that the Bible is "unworthy of belief" **because** of its numerous contradictions and false prophesies (2001). And Dan Barker
(a denominational-preacher-turned-infidel) wrote in his book,
Losing Faith in Faith: "People who are free of theological bias
notice that the bible contains hundreds of discrepancies....
The bible is a flawed book" (1992, pp. 164,177).

Though the Bible has withstood centuries of abuse at the
hands of infidels, the anvil of God's Word rings of the skeptic's blows much more often (and louder) today. Whereas in
the past, the Bible's integrity was attacked only occasionally,
and by people who usually were in the minority, today we live
in a society that is much less "believing." Thomas Paine's denial of biblical truthfulness in the late 18th century led to his
English publisher's imprisonment. Today, Thomas Paine is

hailed as a "scholarly, enlightened freethinker." A century before Paine, a Scottish student named Thomas Aikenhead was hanged for teaching Benedict Spinoza's idea that Moses did not write the Pentateuch (Thiede and D'Ancona, 1996, p. 157). In the 21st century, however, if one does not accept the fundamental principles of Spinoza's theory, he is considered a "nonintellectual" (see Brown, 1999, p. 167). Even when my parents were growing up in the 1940s and 1950s, relatively few people in the United States questioned the existence of God or doubted that the Bible was a special book from God. Yet today, people are asked to believe in the inerrancy of Scripture while living in a much more cynical society. Thus, there is an even greater need to answer the allegations levied against the Bible.

The question concerning alleged discrepancies in the Bible is serious, and it deserves our utmost attention for at least three reasons. First, the doctrine of full or complete inspiration is at stake. By definition, God is perfect, and if the Bible is from God (as it claims to be–2 Timothy 3:16-17; 2 Peter 1:20-21), then it cannot contain contradictions or discrepancies. The Bible is either from God (and thus flawless in its original autographs), or it contains mistakes. There is no middle ground. Second, if there are some errors that are apparent in the Bible, there may be many others that are not. If the Bible contains contradictions, then one could not trust the accounts recorded therein. Third, if the Bible contains contradictions (and thus is not inspired), then the foundation of Christianity is destroyed, since one would be unable to distinguish between what is of man and what is of God. L. Gaussen emphasized the seriousness of this subject when he wrote: "First of all, we acknowledge that, were it true that there were, as they tell us, erroneous facts and contradictory narratives in the Holy Scriptures, one must renounce any attempt to maintain their plenary inspiration" (1949, p. 207). Simply put, if the Word of

God contains legitimate errors, Christianity collapses like a house of cards. And if it is a genuine faith to which Christians cling–faith that is backed by evidence (cf. 1 Peter 3:15)–then the hundreds of alleged contradictions charged to the Bible must be both answerable and answered.

THE KNOW-HOW: PRINCIPLES FOR DEALING WITH ALLEGED CONTRADICTIONS

Innocent Until Proven Guilty

One of the fundamental principles of nearly any study or investigation is that of being "innocent until proven guilty." A teacher cannot justifiably assume that a student who makes a perfect score on a test without studying for it, cheated. It might be that he had received all of the information elsewhere at another time. It could be that he learned everything well enough in class that he did not have to study at home. Or, it may be that he simply "got lucky" and guessed correctly on the questions he did not know. A policeman is not justified in assuming that because a murder was committed by a man wearing green tennis shoes, that the first person the policeman finds wearing green tennis shoes is the murderer.

In our daily lives, we generally consider a person to be truthful until we have evidence that he or she has lied. At the same time, when we read a historical document or book, the same rule should apply. It is considered to be truthful until it can be shown otherwise. A book is to be presumed internally consistent until it can be shown conclusively that it is contradictory. This approach has been accepted throughout literary history, and is still accepted today in most venues. Respected law professor Simon Greenleaf dealt with this principle in his book, *The Testimony of the Evangelists:*

> The rule of municipal law on this subject is familiar, and applies with equal force to all ancient writings, whether documentary or otherwise; and as it comes

first in order, in the prosecution of these inquiries, it
may, for the sake of mere convenience, be designated
as our first rule: "Every document, apparently ancient,
coming from the proper repository or custody, and
bearing on its face no evident marks of forgery, **the
law presumes to be genuine, and devolves on
the opposing party the burden of proving it to
be otherwise**" (1995, p. 16, emp. added).

The accepted way to approach ancient writings is to assume
innocence, not guilt. The Bible deserves this same treatment.

Possibilities Will Suffice

If we believe the Bible is innocent until proven guilty, then
any **possible** answer should be good enough to nullify the
charge of error. This principle does not allow for just **any** answer, but any **possible** answer. When one studies the Bible
and comes across passages that may seem contradictory, one
does not necessarily have to pin down the exact solution in
order to show their truthfulness. The Bible student need only
show the possibility of a harmonization between passages that
appear to conflict in order to negate the force of the charge
that a Bible contradiction really exists.

The alleged contradiction surrounding Mark 2:25-26 illus-
trates the value of this principle. While Jesus and His disciples were strolling through a field one Sabbath, they plucked
ears of grain and ate the kernels. The hypercritical Pharisees
found fault with this act–calling it work–and accused the disciples of breaking the Sabbath law. The Lord responded to
their charge by asking: "Have you never read what David did
when he was in need and hungry, he and those with him: how
he went into the house of God in the days of Abiathar the high
priest, and ate the showbread, which is not lawful to eat, except for the priests, and also gave some to those who were with
him?" Critics compare Christ's reply to 1 Samuel 21 and cry
"Contradiction!"

The difficulty centers on the question over which levitical minister was present when David ate the showbread. Whereas Jesus mentioned **Abiathar**, 1 Samuel 21:1 states: "Then came David to Nob to **Ahimelech** the priest...." Who was correct—Jesus or Samuel? No fewer than three answers are possible. First, it may be that the two names belonged to the same man. Such an answer is not impossible, and finds analogy in Scripture. For example, Moses' father-in-law was known both as Reuel and Jethro (Exodus 2:18; 3:1). And Peter is sometimes called Peter, Simon Peter, Simon, and Cephas (Matthew 14: 28; 16:16; 17:25; John 1:42). It may be that Abiathar and Ahimelech were the same person.

A second possible solution to this "problem" passage may be found in the fact that Jesus did not say Abiathar was the priest who ministered to David, but simply that the event occurred during the lifetime of Abiathar. This is in agreement with 1 Samuel, which mentions a priest named Abiathar several times. Thus, the phrase "in the days of" may not be intended to modify Abiathar's **priesthood**, but his **entire life**.

Third, notice that 1 Samuel does not give the name of the **high** priest when Ahimelech assisted David. Samuel mentioned a **priest** named Ahimelech, whereas Christ mentioned a **high priest** named Abiathar. These were two different offices in the Mosaic age.

Which of these three solutions is correct? Actually, in the absence of more information, a definitive answer seems impossible. However, all of the above answers possess merit. Any one is sufficient to answer the charge of error. Over a century ago, the reputable and conservative Bible scholar J.W. McGarvey commented on this point as follows:

> We are not bound to show the truth of the given hypothesis; but only that it may be true. If it is at all possible, then it is possible that no contradiction exists; if it is probable, then it is probable that no contradic-

tion exists.... It follows, also, that when there is an appearance of contradiction between two writers, **common justice requires that before we pronounce one or both of them false we should exhaust our ingenuity in searching for some probable supposition on the ground of which they may both be true.** The better the general reputation of the writers, the more imperative is this obligation, lest we condemn as false those who are entitled to respectful consideration (1886, part 2, p. 32, emp. added).

Again, the apologist does not have to know the exact solution to an alleged contradiction; he need only show one or more possibilities of harmonization. We act by this principle in the courtroom, in our treatment of various historical books, as well as in everyday-life situations. It is only fair, then, that we show the Bible the same courtesy by exhausting the search for possible harmony between passages before pronouncing one or both accounts false.

What is a Contradiction?

One of the main problems in a discussion concerning alleged contradictions is that most people do not understand what constitutes a genuine contradiction. Ninety-nine percent of all alleged contradictions likely could be resolved simply by acknowledging the real meaning of the word contradiction. What is a contradiction? In its briefest form, the Law of Contradiction, as stated in W. Stanley Jevons' *Elementary Lessons in Logic*, says: "Nothing can both be and not be" (1928, p. 117). The famous Greek philosopher Aristotle amplified this definition by suggesting that there are three areas to which this maxim is applied. He stated: "That the same thing should at the same time both be and not be for the same person and in the same respect is impossible" (see Arndt, 1955, p. x). Although this definition may seem somewhat complicated at first glance, it actually is quite elementary. For example, a door may be open, or a door may be shut, but the same door may not be both open and shut at the same time. With reference to the door, shut and open are opposites, but they are not contradictory unless it be affirmed that they characterize the same object at the same time. So it is very important that one recognizes that mere opposites or differences do not necessitate a contradiction. For there to be a bona fide contradiction, one must be referring to the **same person, place, or thing** in the **same sense** at the **same time**.

Suppose that someone says, "Terry Anthony is rich," and "Terry Anthony is poor." Do those two statements contradict each other? Not necessarily. How do you know the same Terry Anthony is under consideration in both statements? It could be that Terry Anthony in Texas is rich, but Terry Anthony in Tennessee is poor. The same person, place, or thing must be under consideration.

Furthermore, the same time period must be under consideration. Terry Anthony could have made a fortune in his early twenties as a business consultant and been very rich, but after a terrible stock-market crash, he could have lost everything he owned. At one time, then, he was rich, but now he is poor. The two statements could have been accurately describing his life at the time each was made.

Also, the statements must be talking about the same sense. Terry Anthony could have more money than anyone else in the entire world, but if he is not following God, then he is poor. On the other hand, he could have absolutely no money, but be rich in spiritual blessings. After all, "Has God not chosen the poor of this world to be rich in faith" (James 2:5)? Answering these three questions helps tremendously in resolving the contradiction controversy.

These examples reveal that **a mere difference does not make a contradiction**. For a thing both to be and not to be for the same person, place, or thing in the same sense at the same time is a contradiction. But, if it cannot be shown that these three things are all the same, then one cannot honestly say there is a contradiction. It is **never** legitimate to assume a contradiction until every possible means of harmonization has been exhausted.

Consider how the proper understanding of what a contradiction is can help solve allegedly conflicting passages of Scripture.

Same Person, Place, or Thing

The book of Acts records the death of James in Acts 12, while later (Acts 15), James is prominent at the Jerusalem conference. Is this a contradiction? Not at all. The James murdered in Acts 12 was the brother of John (vs. 2), the son of Zebedee (Matthew 4:21), while the James of Acts 15 was Jesus' half-brother (Matthew 13:55; Acts 12:17; 15:13; Galatians 1:19).

Harry Rimmer, author of *The Harmony of Science and Scripture*, wrote about an infidel he knew growing up who once suggested that he had discovered a "contradiction" in the Bible (1936, pp. 193-194). The unbeliever noted that since Noah's ark (described in Genesis 6) was 300 cubits long, fifty cubits wide, and thirty cubits high (or 450 feet x 75 feet x 45 feet) and would have weighed several tons when fully loaded, it was preposterous to believe that the priests could have carried it across the Jordan River as described in Joshua 3! Impossible, right? A clear-cut contradiction? The critic's inability to distinguish between the **ark of Noah** and the **ark of the covenant** made answering his argument a simple matter for even the most elementary Bible student. Obviously, different objects were under consideration. The priests carried the ark of the covenant–not the ark of Noah (cf. Genesis 6: 14-16; Exodus 25:10-15). It is critically important, first, to make sure that differences between two or more passages are not the result of different people, places, or things being discussed.

Same Time Reference

Some time ago, I visited a skeptic's Web site in which he indicated that Genesis 1:31 and Genesis 6:5-6 were contradictory. Supposedly, a discrepancy is evident since in Genesis 1 the Bible records, "Then God saw everything that He had made, and indeed it was very good," and then in Genesis 6 it says, "And the Lord was sorry that He had made man on the earth, and He was grieved in His heart." The Lord could not be both satisfied and dissatisfied with His creation, could He? He certainly could—if the statements were not referring to the same time. It just so happens that the events, though only five chapters apart in the Bible, are separated—chronologically speaking—by hundreds of years.

Another skeptic charged the Bible with making a mistake after comparing Genesis 6:9 with Genesis 9:21. In the first verse, Noah is described as being "a just man, perfect in his generations." In the second passage, Noah's drunkenness is described. How is it that Noah could be "a just man," while also being a drunk? The same person, admittedly, is under consideration in both passages. The problem with this line of reasoning is that the two verses are separated by more than one hundred years. Furthermore, one also would be incorrect in concluding from Genesis 9 that Noah was a drunkard. He may have continued to "walk with God" throughout his life, despite his struggles with sin (cf. Hebrews 11:7,13).

Same Sense

If any book is to be understood correctly, it is imperative that recognition be given to the different senses in which words may be used. For example, in Philippians 3:12 Paul wrote that he had not yet been "made perfect" (ASV), but then, just three verses later, he indicated that he was "perfect." How do we harmonize Paul's denial of perfection in verse 12 with his affirmation in verse 15 that he was perfect? The former "perfection" is a faultlessness and excellence that cannot be expected in this life. Paul had not yet attained a state of total holiness and dedication when no additional progress would be possible or needed. The "perfection" or "maturity" of verse 15 was "used to mean mature in mind, as opposed to one who is a beginner in a subject" (Barclay, 1959, p. 81).

Normally, terms are used literally, but they sometimes can be employed figuratively as well. In Matthew 11:14, Jesus referred to John the Baptist as "Elijah," yet on another occasion the forerunner of Christ plainly denied that he was Elijah (John 1:21). These verses are reconciled quite easily when we recognize that even though John was not **literally** Elijah (physically reincarnated), he was the **spiritual antitype** of that great prophet. He prepared the way for Christ "in the spirit and power of Elijah" (Luke 1:17).

On occasion, a biblical passage also may appear to be in conflict with a historical fact because it employs language in a different sense than the way we normally use it. Such likely is the case with Daniel 2:39. In this passage (2:31-45), Daniel was interpreting Nebuchadnezzar's prophetic dream. The most widely accepted view of the interpretation of Nebuchadnezzar's dream, which is backed by a vast amount of historical and archaeological evidence, is that the gold, silver, brass, and iron/clay sections of the statue refer respectively to the Babylonian, Medo-Persian, Greek, and Roman empires. Since Daniel stated that the second kingdom (representing the Medo-Persian Empire) would be "inferior" (2:39) to the first (Babylon), critics claim that Daniel was historically inaccurate since the Medo-Persian Empire was larger and richer than the Babylonian Empire. Surely Daniel would not refer to a kingdom as being **inferior** when it was larger than the one spoken of as being **superior**.

Could Daniel have been referring to the second kingdom, and therefore been using the term "inferior" in a different sense than the way we most frequently use the word? Most certainly. Keep in mind that the reference to the second kingdom being inferior does not mean that it necessarily was inferior in all respects. H.C. Leupold mentioned the fact that the Persian Empire was inferior in the sense of influence on the rest of the world. Babylonian culture was dominant in that part of the world for around 2,000 years, and is well known for many of its accomplishments in architecture and science (1989, p. 116). The truth is, in Daniel 2:39, the prophet never mentioned **what** was inferior about the second kingdom; rather, he merely stated that **something** would be inferior. The key to understanding this supposed historical discrepancy (and many others) is to understand that the writer used the word in a different sense than the way we most often think of it.

Supplementation Does not Equal Contradiction

Another common-sense principle that is useful in approaching alleged contradictions relates to one's understanding of supplementation. Suppose you are telling a story about the time you and a friend went to an Atlanta Braves baseball game. You mention what great defense the Braves played, and your friend tells about their clutch hits in the final innings of the game. Is there a contradiction just because your friend mentions the Braves' offense but you mention only the defense? No. He is simply adding to (or supplementing) your story to make it more complete. That happens in the Bible quite often.

As an example, in Matthew 14:21 the Bible says that Jesus fed about five thousand men, and that He also fed women and children. But in Mark 6:44, it says that He fed about five thousand men. Mark never mentions the women and children. Is that a contradiction? No, of course not. Did Jesus feed about 5,000 men? Yes, and that makes Mark correct. Did Jesus break the loaves for about 5,000 men, along with some women and children? Yes, which makes Matthew right, too. Just because one account "adds" some things does not mean that the accounts contradict each other.

Again, Matthew 27:57-60 says that Joseph of Arimathea took Jesus' body and placed it in his tomb, yet John 19:38-40 says that Joseph **and Nicodemus** put the body in the tomb. Do they contradict each other? Certainly not! If one text said **only** Joseph did it or **only** Nicodemus did it, then a contradiction might exist. But as it stands, John simply "adds" some facts to the story. Supplementary accounts are not contradictory.

Look Who's Talking

Another principle that must be remembered when dealing with various biblical passages is that the Bible reports numerous uninspired statements. Even though "all Scripture is given by inspiration of God" (2 Timothy 3:16), not everything that the inspired writers recorded was a true statement. For example, after God created Adam, He told him not to eat of the tree of the knowledge of good and evil lest he die (Genesis 2:17). Yet, when the serpent approached Eve, he "informed" her that she would **not** die if she ate of this forbidden fruit (3:4). Obviously, Satan was not inspired by God to say, "You will not surely die." In fact, as we learn later, he actually lied (John 8:44). However, when Moses recorded the events that took place in Eden hundreds of years later, he wrote by inspiration of God (cf. Luke 24:44; John 5:46). When Jesus healed a demoniac, some of the Pharisees accused Him of casting out demons, not by the power of God, but by the power of "Beelzebub, the ruler of the demons" (Matthew 12:24). Like Moses, Matthew did not lie, but merely reported a lie. The writers of the Bible are in no way responsible for the inaccurate statements that are recorded therein. Whether the statements were true or false, they reported them accurately.

The above examples are quite basic: Satan's statement and the Pharisees' allegations clearly were false. But what about instances where statements are made by individuals who do not seem "as bad" as these? I once read an article by a gentleman who was defending a doctrine by citing various verses in the book of Job. The problem was that these verses blatantly contradicted other passages in the Bible. This man was mistaken in his understanding of the biblical text because he never took into consideration one of the fundamental rules of interpretation—knowing who is speaking; he simply cited all statements as being true. One who studies the book of Job must realize that it is an inspired book that contains many **un**inspired statements. For instance, we know that Job's wife was incorrect when she told him to "curse God and die" (Job 2:9). We also know that many statements made by Eliphaz, Bildad, and Zophar were incorrect. Nine of the forty-two chapters in the book were speeches by these "miserable comforters" (16:2) whom God said had "not spoken of Me what is right, as My servant Job has" (42:7). Clearly, then, one never should quote these men and claim the statement as an inspired truth (unless, of course, an inspired man verified it as being true—cf. 1 Corinthians 3:19).

The Golden Rule

A final rule to keep in mind when interpreting alleged contradictory passages is that we need to be as fair with the Bible as we wish others to be toward us. Suppose you mentioned to a friend at work that you woke up at sunrise. How would you feel if your coworker responded by saying, "You are a moron. The Sun does not rise! That's just the Earth rotating on its axis."? No doubt, you would think this person had some serious problems, because it is common knowledge that the Sun does not literally rise in the east; however, people have no problem understanding the real meaning of this comment. We call this "phenomenal" language—language that is used in everyday speech to refer to ordinary phenomena. On occasion, the Bible also uses phenomenal language. In Psalm 50:1, the writer described the Sun as rising, and in 1 Corinthians 15:6 Paul described some of the Christians who had died as having "fallen asleep." No one would accuse us of making a scientific mistake when we say that the Sun will rise, or that a dead person has "fallen asleep." In the same way, the Bible should not be accused of containing mistakes simply because it uses the same type of language. So, remember, the Bible regularly describes things as they appear—rather than in scientific terms—just as you do in casual conversation.

Having set forth these nine foundational principles, the groundwork is complete. Let us now turn our attention to answering many of the alleged contradictions and/or discrepancies that skeptics have proposed as insurmountable.

Chapter 2

ALLEGED CONTRADICTIONS IN THE CREATION ACCOUNT

TOO MUCH ACTIVITY ON DAY SIX?

Genesis 2:18-20

One of the reasons infidelic scoffers reject the validity of the biblical account of creation is because they find it impossible to believe that one man could name every single species of animal on the Earth in a single day. Considering that there are only 86,400 seconds in a 24-hour period, we are told it is ludicrous to believe that an individual (who had never seen animals before the day he named them) could name several million species of animals in one day. Perhaps over a period of a few weeks he might accomplish such a task, but certainly not in a single day–right?

The problem with such objections to Genesis 2:18-20 is that they are based on assumptions. The question that skeptics often ask, "Could Adam have gathered and named all of the animals on the Earth in one day?," is misleading because the Bible places certain restrictions on the animals Adam named. Consider the following.

- Adam's task did not include searching for and gathering all of God's creatures. Rather, God "brought them" to him (Genesis 2:19). Likely this was in some sort of orderly fashion in order to reduce the amount of time and human energy necessary to complete the process.

- Genesis 2:20 does not say that Adam named "all" of the animals on the Earth. The text actually says, "Adam gave names to all cattle, to the birds of the air, and to every beast of the field." Excluded from this naming process were sea creatures and creeping things mentioned earlier in the creation narrative (cf. Genesis 1: 21,25).

- The beasts God brought to Adam are qualified by the descriptive phrase "of the field" (*hassadeh*). Although the precise limits of the term "field" are difficult to determine, it is possible that it refers only to those beasts living in Eden.

- If the beasts of the field were limited to those animals within the boundaries of Eden, then livestock and birds could have been similarly limited. This would greatly reduce the number of animals involved in the naming process, since it is very unlikely that all created animals lived in Eden. [If so, Eden might have been quickly overrun and destroyed.]

- Contrary to popular belief, Adam did not name millions of **species** of animals on day six (cf. Wells, 2001; McKinsey, 2000, p. 84). Genesis 1 states that the animals were created "according to their kind(s)" (vs. 21), not species. The Bible was written long before man invented the Linnaean classification system. The "kinds" (Hebrew *min*) of animals Adam named on the sixth day of creation were probably very broad—more like groups of birds and land animals rather than specific genera and species. Adam would have given animals general names like "turtle," "dog," or "elephant," not special names like "pig-nosed soft-shell turtle" or "Alaskan Husky."

All of these textual considerations suggest that the events of day six could have been accomplished easily within a 24-hour period. Adam did not have to spend a great deal of time pondering what he would call each animal; he was created with the ability to speak and reason. If my oldest son, when he was two years old, could look at a book and call the names of sixty different **kinds** of animals in sixty seconds, I have no problem believing that Adam, having been created directly by the hand of God and made in His image (see Lyons and Thompson, 2002), had the ability to name hundreds (if not thousands) of birds and land animals in 3,600 seconds (just one hour!). [Various authors have documented how it would be quite possible for Adam to have named large numbers of animals in a very short period of time. The interested reader is referred to: (a) Morris, 1976, pp. 96-98; and (b) Thompson, 2000, pp. 205-210.]

[NOTE: Some Bible believers may answer the question regarding the length of day six by simply saying, "We don't know how long the days of creation were. They could have been long periods of time, thus giving Adam all the time he needed to name the animals." However, the available evidence (**of which the skeptic is very aware**) reveals several reasons why we can know that the days mentioned in Genesis 1 are the same kind of days we experience in the present age, and were not eons of time. The Bible states that the heavens, the Earth, the sea and **all** that is in them were created in six days (Exodus 20:8-11; 31:17; Genesis 1). Genesis 1:5 even states that each of these days was a period of "evening and morning" so that there would be no doubt as to the length of each of the creation days. (The words "evening" and "morning" are used together in the Old Testament with the word *yom* over 100 times in non-prophetic passages, and each time they refer to a 24-hour day.) Additionally, we are told in Genesis 1:14 that the lights in the heavens were "for signs, for seasons, and for days, and years." If the days that are described by "evening and morning" were long epochs of time, then what were the "years"? Indeed, God could have created the Universe in any amount of time He chose. The point is, however, He said He did it in six days, not six long periods of time (cf. Exodus 20:8-11; Mark 10:6; Romans 1:20-21).]

DID GOD CREATE
ANIMALS OR MAN FIRST?
Genesis 1:24-27; 2:18-19

The amount of time it took Adam to name the animals God brought to him on day six is not the only problem that skeptics have with this particular day of creation. While Genesis 1:24-27 plainly indicates that man was created **after** the animals, it is claimed that Genesis 2:18-19 teaches that man was created **before** animals. Skeptics strongly assert that such language by the author of Genesis proves that the Bible is not divinely inspired.

Does Genesis 2 present a different creation order than Genesis 1? Is there a reasonable explanation for the differences between the two chapters? Or is this to be recognized as a genuine contradiction?

Some Bible students resolve this alleged contradiction simply by explaining that the Hebrew verb translated "formed" could easily have been translated "had formed." In his *Exposition of Genesis*, Herbert Leupold stated:

> Without any emphasis on the sequence of acts the account here records the making of the various creatures and the bringing of them to man. That in real-

ity they had been made prior to the creation of man is so entirely apparent from chapter one as not to require explanation. But the reminder that God had "molded" them makes obvious His power to bring them to man and so is quite appropriately mentioned here. It would not, in our estimation, be wrong to translate *yatsar* as a pluperfect in this instance: "He had molded." The insistence of the critics upon a plain past is partly the result of the attempt to make chapters one and two clash at as many points as possible (1942, p. 130).

Hebrew scholar Victor Hamilton agreed with Leupold's assessment of Genesis 2:19 as he also recognized that "it is possible to translate formed as 'had formed' " (1990, p. 176). Keil and Delitzsch stated in the first volume of their highly regarded Old Testament commentary that "our modern style for expressing the same thought [which the Holy Spirit via Moses intended to communicate—EL] would be simply this: 'God brought to Adam the beasts which He **had** formed' " (1996). Adding even more credence to this interpretation is the fact that the New International Version renders the verb in verse 19, not as simple past tense, but as a pluperfect: "Now the Lord God **had formed** out of the ground all the beasts of the field and all the birds of the air." Although Genesis 1 and 2 agree even when *yatsar* is translated simply "formed" (as we will notice in the remainder of this section), it is important to note that the four Hebrew scholars mentioned above, and the translators of the NIV, all believe that it **could** (or should) be rendered "had formed." As Leupold acknowledged, those who deny this possibility do so (at least partly) because of their insistence on making the two chapters disagree.

The main reason that skeptics do not see harmony in the events recorded in the first two chapters of the Bible (especially regarding the order of God's creation—whether vege-

tation, birds, land animals, man, etc.) is because they fail to
realize that **Genesis 1 and 2 serve different purposes**. Chapter one (including 2:1-4) focuses on the **order** of the creation
events; chapter two (actually 2:5-25) simply provides more
detailed information about some of the events mentioned in
chapter one. Chapter two never was meant to be a regurgita-
tion of chapter one, but instead serves its own unique purpose—
to develop in detail the more important features of the creation account, especially the creation of man and his surroundings. As Kenneth Kitchen noted in his book, *Ancient Orient
and the Old Testament*:

> Genesis 1 mentions the creation of man as the last of
> a series, and without any details, whereas in Genesis
> 2 man is the center of interest and more specific de-
> tails are given about him and his setting. Failure to
> recognize the complementary nature of the subject-
> distinction between a skeleton outline of all creation
> on the one hand, and the concentration in detail on
> man and his immediate environment on the other,
> borders on obscurantism (1966, p. 117).

Norman Geisler and Thomas Howe summarized some of the
differences in Genesis 1-2 in the following chart (1992, p. 35):

Genesis 1	Genesis 2
Chronological order	Topical order
Outline	Details
Creating animals	Naming animals

The fact is, "Genesis 2 does not present a creation account at
all but presupposes the completion of God's work of creation
as set forth in chapter 1.... [C]hapter 2 is built on the foundation of chapter 1 and represents no different tradition than
the first chapter or discrepant account of the order of crea-

tion" (Archer, 1982, pp. 68-69). In short, Genesis 1 and 2 are harmonious in every way. What may seem as a contradiction at first glance is essentially a more detailed account of chapter one. The text of Genesis 2:19 says nothing about the relative origins of man and beast in terms of chronology, but merely suggests that the animals were formed before being brought to man.

If one still rejects both the possibility of *yatsar* being translated "had formed," and the explanation of the two chapters being worded differently because of the purposes they serve, a final response to the skeptic's allegations is that the text never says that there were no animals created on the sixth day of creation **after** Adam. Although in my judgment it is **very unlikely** that God created a special group of animals to be named by Adam (after creating all others before the creation of man–Genesis 1:20-27), some commentators hold this view. After his comments concerning the translation of *yatsar*, Victor Hamilton indicated that the creatures mentioned in 2:19 refer "to the creation of **a special group** of animals brought before Adam for naming" (p. 176, emp. added). Hamilton believes that most all the animals on the Earth were created before Adam; however, those mentioned in 2:19 were created on day six after Adam for the purpose of being named. In U. Cassuto's comments on Genesis 2 regarding the time Adam named the animals, he stated: "Of all the species of beasts and flying creatures that had been created and had spread over the face of the earth and the firmament of the heavens, the Lord God **now** formed particular specimens for the purpose of presenting them all before man in the midst of the Garden" (1961, p. 129, emp. added). Both of these long-time Bible students recognize that the text never says there were no animals created after Adam, but that all animals were created either on days five and six (before and possibly even after Adam was created). However unorthodox (and unlikely) this position may be, it does serve as another reason why skeptics have no foundation upon which to stand when they assert that a contradiction exists between 1:24-27 and 2:19.

OF WATER OR OF LAND?

Genesis 1:20-22; 2:19

In what appears to be skeptics "grasping for straws," one of their latest allegations has been to assert that a contradiction exists between Genesis 1:20-22 and 2:19. Allegedly, 1:20-22 teaches that birds were formed out of the **water**, whereas 2:19 teaches that they were formed out of the **ground**.

The simple fact of the matter is that those who claim such a contradiction exists have misquoted the text and misunderstood its wording. We readily admit that Genesis 2:19 teaches that "out of the ground the Lord God formed every beast of the field and every bird of the air." However, contrary to skeptics' accusations, Genesis 1:20-22 does not contradict this statement. Rather, it reads:

> Then God said, "Let the waters abound (swarm, ASV) with an abundance of living creatures, and let birds fly above the earth across the face of the firmament of the heavens." So God created great sea creatures and every living thing that moves, with which the waters abounded, according to their kind, and every winged bird according to its kind... And God blessed them, saying, "Be fruitful and multiply, and fill the waters in the seas, and let birds multiply on the earth."

Where does this passage say that birds were formed from the water? It does not. It simply teaches that God caused some living creatures to appear in the water, and He caused birds to fly above the Earth. This passage does not teach that the waters were the **cause** of the fish, but the **element** of the fish, just as the air is the element of the birds (Barnes, 1997).

[NOTE: Bible scholars and apologists consider this "alleged Bible contradiction" such a lame attempt to disprove the Bible's inspiration that relatively few have even bothered responding to it. Surely, at some point in time, common sense will allow everyone to see the shallowness of the critics' accusations. The only reason this refutation has been included here is so that those who are contemplating the Bible's inerrancy will not blindly swallow the critics' allegations (as many have done) without first carefully reading what the passage says and what it does not say.]

IS MARRIAGE A GOOD THING?
Genesis 2:18; 1 Corinthians 7:1,7-8,26

Generally, marriage is looked upon by the world around us as a good and honorable institution. Since the commencement of time, the universal law has been that marriage is proper and beneficial. On the very day God created the first man, He stated: "It is not good that man should be alone" (Genesis 2:18); thus He created a wife for Adam (2:21-24). Everything God created and examined up until this point had been "good" (1:4,10,21,25). The one thing He stated as being "not good," however, was man's lack of human companionship. Thus, God created the woman to be man's helper and lifelong companion. It was only after her creation (at the end of the six days) that we read for the first time His creation was "very good" (1:31).

Although other biblical passages confirm that "marriage is honorable among all" (Hebrews 13:4), and that "he who finds a wife finds a good thing" (Proverbs 18:22), some have questioned the reliability of the creation account in light of Paul's assessment of marriage in his first letter to the Corinthian church. In this epistle he wrote the following:

"It is good for a man not to touch a woman" (7:1).

"I wish that all men were even as I myself [i.e., not married–EL]" (7:7).

"I say to the unmarried and to the widows: It is good
for them if they remain even as I am" (7:8).

"It is good for a man to remain as he is" (7:26).

Allegedly, Paul's analysis of marriage is in opposition to the
view found in the creation account. Whereas God said, "It is
not good that man should be alone" (Genesis 2:18, emp.
added), Paul told the Corinthian church that "It **is** good" to
remain single. Can these two views of marriage be reconciled?
Or is this a legitimate contradiction?

As is often the case, the verses in 1 Corinthians only present a problem because the context of chapter 7 has been overlooked. The reader must understand that Paul is responding
to questions he received in a letter from the Corinthians (7:
1). Obviously, some of the questions pertained to marriage,
and whether or not the apostle deemed it advisable. What
many people overlook is that the questions were asked, and
Paul's responses were given, in light of "the present distress"
that the Corinthians were facing. Likely, the church at Corinth had asked him whether or not it was proper for a Christian to marry in their present circumstances. In 7:26 Paul wrote:
"I suppose therefore that this is good **because of the present distress**–that it is good for a man to remain as he is [sin-
gle–EL]" (emp. added). Exactly what "the present distress"
was at this time is unknown, but it likely involved oppression
and persecution at the hands of the Romans (possibly Emperor
Nero).

Whatever the precise "distress" was in Corinth, it is clear
that God inspired Paul to write that it was in the Christians'
best interest to remain unmarried. Perhaps he wanted to spare
them situations like someone telling them they must either
deny Christ or see a family member put to death (cf. Jeremiah
16:1-4). Even today, if a person is aware that severe persecution is imminent, he likely will delay getting married and having children. When Jesus spoke about the "great distress" that

would come upon Jerusalem, He specifically warned "those who are pregnant" and "those who are nursing babies" (Luke 21:23). Jesus informed them that they would have greater difficulties surviving "the edge of the sword" that would come upon Jerusalem (Luke 21:24; cf. Matthew 24:19-21). Similarly, Paul advised those in Corinth to remain unmarried "because of the present distress" (1 Corinthians 7:26).

The Bible's teaching on marriage is clear to the unbiased reader: marriage "is honorable among all" (Hebrews 13:4), and since the beginning it normally has been "good" for mankind (Genesis 2:18). In some cases, however, it might become inadvisable. In 1 Corinthians 7, Paul simply mentioned one such case.

WHY DIDN'T ADAM DIE IMMEDIATELY?

Genesis 2:16-17; 5:5

In the Garden of Eden, the Lord delivered a single, solemn prohibition to man. God commanded Adam saying, "Of every tree of the garden you may freely eat; but of the tree of the knowledge of good and evil you shall not eat, **for in the day that you eat of it you shall surely die**" (Genesis 2:16-17, emp. added). The tree of the knowledge of good and evil that stood in the midst of the garden was off limits to Adam and Eve. God prophesied that disobedience on their part would bring death "in the day" it was eaten. However, the Genesis text does not reveal an instantaneous, physical death on the part of the first sinners. Adam lived a total of 930 years (Genesis 5:5), and the text indicates that most of those occurred **after** the transgression in the Garden of Eden (see Thompson, 2002, 22:44-46). Is such consistent with Genesis 2:16-17? Was God mistaken in saying, "in the day that you eat of it [the fruit–EL] you shall surely die"? Why is it that Adam did not drop dead the very day he ate of the forbidden fruit?

For Genesis 2:17 to represent a legitimate contradiction, one first would have to assume that the phrase "**in the day**...you shall surely die" must refer to an **immediate** death occurring on the very day a certain transgression has taken place. The available evidence shows, however, that the Hebrew idiom *bᵉyôm* ("in the day") refers to the **certainty** of death, not the **immediacy** of it. For example, King Solomon once warned a subversive Shimei: "For it shall be, **on the day** (*bᵉyôm*) you go out and cross the Brook Kidron, know for certain you shall surely die; your blood shall be on your own head" (1 Kings 2: 37). As the next few verses indicate, Shimei could not have been executed on the exact day he crossed the Brook Kidron. Solomon did not call for him until after Shimei had saddled his donkey, went to king Achish at Gath, sought and retrieved his slaves, and returned home (approximately a 50-60 mile round trip). It is logical to conclude that this would have taken more than just one day (especially considering a donkey's average journey was only about 20 miles a day–Cansdale, 1996, p. 38). It was only after Shimei's return from Gath that King Solomon reminded him of his promise saying, "Did I not make you swear by the Lord, and warn you, saying, 'Know for certain that **on the day** you go out and travel anywhere, you shall surely die?' " (1 Kings 2:42, emp. added). Solomon understood that even though he executed Shimei sometime after the day he crossed Brook Kidron, it still was proper to refer to it as occurring "on the day." As Hebrew scholar Victor Hamilton noted, this phrase (in Genesis 2:17; 1 Kings 2:37,42; and Exodus 10: 28ff.) "is underscoring the certainty of death, not its chronology" (1990, p. 172). Thus, it is logical to conclude that when God said, "in the day...you shall surely die," He did not mean Adam would die on the exact day of his transgression, but that his death would be **certain** if he ate of the forbidden fruit.

A second problem with the skeptic's assertion that Genesis 2:17 contradicts 5:5 is that it assumes the "death" mentioned in 2:17 is a physical death. The Bible, however, describes three different kinds of "deaths": (1) a physical death that ends our life on Earth (Genesis 35:18); (2) a spiritual death, which is separation from God (Isaiah 59:1-2; Ephesians 2:1); and (3) an eternal death in hell (Revelation 21:8). The fact is, one cannot know for sure what death is indicated by the phrase, "for in the day that you eat of it you will surely die." Realizing that Adam sinned against the Almighty in the garden, and thus became "dead in trespasses and sins" (Ephesians 2:1; cf. 1 Timothy 5:6), it is more than possible that the death spoken of in Genesis 2:17 is a spiritual death. If this is the case, the reason Adam did not **physically** drop dead on the very day of his transgression was because God's prophecy was referring to a **spiritual** death, not a physical one.

There is, however, another possible explanation to Adam's prolonged life span that is worthy of consideration. On several occasions, God reversed His previously stated will regarding specific circumstances (cf. Genesis 18:16-33; Jonah 3:1-10). Compelled by His mercy, God occasionally suspended His judgment, suffering long with His rebellious creation. Such possibly was the case with Adam and Eve. If this interpretation of Genesis 2:17 is correct, God did not require them to pay the full penalty for their transgression, but instead set in motion a redemptive plan (cf. Ephesians 3:11) in which He accepted a substitutionary sacrifice for sin. In Adam and Eve's case, it might be that the animals from which God made the skins to clothe their naked bodies represented the first sin offering (Genesis 3:21). At any rate, the punishment articulated for Adam and Eve's sin has implications in a broader spiritual sense. The punishment for Adam's sin (and that of all humankind) was paid by Jesus. The price Jesus paid involved a physical death, and thus the punishment for Adam's sin (and all humankind) involved a physical death.

When Adam chose to follow his own desires instead of God's will, he cut himself off from God. Without a doubt, man perished spiritually on that day. But equally certain is the fact that God's punishment for that sin was a physical death—a death that, for Adam, would occur centuries later. Furthermore, when Adam and Eve sinned, God set in motion the redemptive plan that eventually demanded His own Son's incarnate death. Truly, Adam and Eve's sin resulted in three "deaths." Exactly which death God meant for us to understand in Genesis 2:17 is uncertain, and thus a dogmatic stance is inappropriate.

[NOTE: One might be curious as to how the term "day" (Hebrew *yom*) in Genesis 2:17 and 1 Kings 2:37 could possibly refer to something more than a literal 24-hour period, if it could not be interpreted thusly in reference to the days of creation in Genesis 1. The fact is, the Hebrew word for day has several different meanings. It can refer to that which is opposite of night (Genesis 1:5); it can refer to a period of time in the future, such as the "day of judgment" (1 John 4:17) or "the day" Shimei would die (1 Kings 2:37,42); it is used in Genesis 2:4 to refer to the **total** of the six days of creation; and it can mean a literal twenty-four hours. One key to defining this word, as well as all words, is to look at it within its context. The usage of "day" (*yom*) in regard to the days of creation demands a 24-hour interpretation. The usage of "day" (*yom*) in Genesis 2:17 is less clear and could mean "a period of time in the future."]

WHERE DID CAIN GET HIS WIFE?

Genesis 4:16-17

Many infidels and skeptics have used this apparent inconsistency as evidence for the allegorical or mythological nature of the early Genesis record, in opposition to plain historicity as advocated by biblical conservatives. While it is true the Bible is not specific on this matter, there is no difficulty in suggesting a reasonable solution that does no violence to scriptural interpretation.

The most common solution is to propose that Cain married a near relative—perhaps a sister. Initially this may seem to be a radical idea, but as we will note, it is the most realistic option. We are told in specific terms that Adam and Eve had three sons—Cain, Abel, and sometime later, Seth. However, we also are told that Adam was the father of "other sons and daughters" (Genesis 5:4). Eve had given birth to Cain and Abel soon after leaving Eden (Genesis 4:1-2), but she could have had other children between their birth and Abel's death, and between that murder and the birth of Seth. In any case, one female offspring could later have become Cain's wife. [Some have inquired as to whether or not Cain could have married someone else not of Adam and Eve's family—viz., a woman of other people whom God had created. In light of Scripture, this is not a possibility. The Bible makes it plain that Eve was the "mother of **all** living" (Genesis 3:20). If Adam was the first man (1 Corinthians 15:45), and if Eve was the mother of **all**, then it is clear that there were no "other people" left for Cain to marry. The population of the Earth came directly through the lineage of Adam and Eve.]

Many people immediately see a problem with marriages that must, of necessity, be incestuous in nature. Remember, however, that incest itself was outlawed only with the coming of the Mosaic covenant (Leviticus 18). There was no need for strict laws on marriage partners in the early Patriarchal Age (apart from the divine "one man, one woman, for life" institution—Genesis 2:24) for at least one good reason: during this time, man was in a relatively pure state, physically speaking, having recently left the perfect condition in which he was created, and the garden that had sustained his life. Adam and Eve could have lived forever had it not been for their corruption by sin, and their consequent expulsion from Eden (Genesis 3:1-6). Hence, no harmful genetic traits had emerged at this point that could have been expressed in the children of closely related partners. However, after many generations, and especially after the Noahic Flood (Genesis 6-9), solar and cosmic radiation, chemical and viral mutagens, and DNA replication errors, led to the multiplication of various genetic disorders. God protected His people by instituting, in the eighteenth chapter of Leviticus, strict laws against incestuous marriages. Needless to say, more genetic disorders have arisen in the world population since the time of Moses, and thus it is even more important to avoid marrying a close relative. Christianity thus far has ensured that such rules have been carried forward into modern laws in the western world.

WHAT ABOUT THE LAND OF NOD?
Genesis 4:16-17

After Cain killed Abel and was declared a "fugitive and vagabond" by God (Genesis 4:12), the Bible says that he "went out from the presence of the Lord and dwelt in the land of Nod" (4:16). It was in this land that "Cain knew his wife" (4:17), and it was here that his son, Enoch, was born.

When a person reads about Nod in Genesis 4, he often pictures a land where a large group of people already was dwelling by the time Cain arrived. Because the Bible gives this land a name ("Nod"), many assume it was called such before Cain went there. Furthermore, many believe that it was in this land that Cain found his wife. Based upon these assumptions, some even claim that God must have specially created additional humans besides Adam and Eve, otherwise there would not have been a land of Nod, nor would Cain have been able to find a wife there. Are these assumptions and conclusions correct?

It is very likely that when Moses wrote the name "Nod" (Genesis 4:16), he was using a literary device known as "prolepsis" (the assignment of something, such as an event or name, to a time that precedes it). People often use prolepsis for the sake of convenience, so that the reader or audience can better understand what is being communicated. For example, I might say, "My wife and I dated two years before we got married," when actually she was not my wife when we were dating, but a very dear friend. We may see a special on television about when President Ronald Reagan was a boy, but the fact is, Ronald Reagan was not President of the United States when he was a boy. From time to time, even the Bible uses this kind of language. In John 11, the Bible speaks of a woman named Mary who "anointed the Lord with ointment" (11:1-2), yet this anointing actually did not occur for about three months. John merely spoke about it as having already happened because when he wrote his gospel account, this event was generally known. Another example of prolepsis is found in Genesis 13: 3 where we read that Abraham "went on his journey from the South as far as Bethel." This area actually did not wear the name Bethel until years later when Jacob gave it that name (Genesis 28:19). However, when Moses wrote of this name hundreds of years later, he was free to use it even when writing about a time before the name actually was given.

When Moses, writing around 1500 B.C., used the name Nod in Genesis 4, the reader must understand the land probably was not given that name until sometime **after** Cain moved there. This is consistent with the meaning of the name Nod ("wandering"), which in all probability was given because God told Cain he was to be a wanderer upon the Earth (Genesis 4: 12). Thus, the land of Nod almost certainly was not an area filled with people whom Cain might eventually befriend. It might have become that in time; nevertheless, it probably was not such a place upon his arrival.

But, someone might ask, did Cain not find his wife in the land of Nod? Actually, the Bible never tells us that Cain's wife came from Nod. The text simply says that Cain "dwelt in the land of Nod on the east of Eden. And Cain knew his wife, and she conceived and bore Enoch" (Genesis 4:16-17).

To conclude that God specially created others besides Adam and Eve because "there was a large group of people living in Nod when Cain arrived," and that "from this group Cain got his wife," is faulty reasoning. Scripture does not teach the above premises, nor does it ever suggest that God specially created others than Adam and Eve. In fact, the Bible teaches the very opposite when it makes plain that Adam was the first man (1 Corinthians 15:45), and that Eve would be the mother of **all** living (Genesis 3:20).

Chapter 3

DID MOSES WRITE THE PENTATEUCH?

Some time ago, a young lady from a local university visited our offices at Apologetics Press and requested to speak to someone about a "new theory" she had been taught in her freshmen literature class. For the first time in her life, she had been told that Moses could not have been the author of the first five books of the Old Testament.

> "*He lived too early in human history to have written it.*"
>
> "*The Pentateuch contains information Moses could not have known.*"
>
> "*Many of the details are from a later age inappropriately inserted into Genesis.*"
>
> "*The Pentateuch actually was pieced together by anonymous sources (commonly called J, E, D, and P) at a fairly late date—long after Moses' death.*"

This impressionable young freshman was extremely disturbed by her professor's statements. She was taken aback by the things skeptics and "biblical scholars" had to say about the matter. Consequently, she began to question what she had learned regarding the Mosaic authorship of the Pentateuch

in her Sunday school classes and at the Christian school she
had attended nearly all of her life.

> "*Why would I be taught my whole life by teachers and preach-
> ers that Moses wrote Genesis through Deuteronomy, if he
> really didn't?*"

> "*Why did I not know about this until now?*"

> "*Does it really matter who wrote Genesis, anyway?*"

THE DOCUMENTARY HYPOTHESIS

The idea that Moses did not write the Pentateuch actually
has been around for more than a millennium. However, until the mid-seventeenth century, the vast majority of people
still maintained that Moses was its author. It was in the mid-
1600s that the Dutch philosopher Benedict Spinoza began se-
riously to question this widely held belief (Green, 1978, p. 47;
Dillard and Longman, 1994, p. 40). French physician Jean
Astruc developed the original Documentary Hypothesis in
1753, which went through many different alterations until Karl
Graf revised the original hypothesis in the mid-nineteenth century. Julius Wellhausen then restated Graf's Documentary
Hypothesis and brought it to light in European and American scholarly circles (McDowell, 1999, pp. 404-406). It has
become known to many as the Graf-Wellhausen Hypothesis.

Since the "period of Enlightenment," the Graf-Wellhausen
explanation of the origin of the Pentateuch has been thrust
consistently into the faces of Christians. Liberal scholars teach
that the Pentateuch was compiled from four original source
documents–designated as J, E, D, and P. These four documents
supposedly were written at different times by different authors,
and eventually were compiled into the Pentateuch by a redac-
tor (editor). The J, or Jehovahist, document (usually known
as the Yahwehist document) supposedly was written around
850 B.C. and was characterized by its use of the divine name
Yahweh. Elohim is the divine name that identifies the E, or Elohist,

document, purportedly written around 750 B.C. The D, or Deuteronomist, document contained most of the book of Deuteronomy and was supposed to have been written around 620 B.C. The last section to be written was the P, or Priestly, document, which would have contained most of the priestly laws, and allegedly was written around 500 B.C. We are told these documents were then redacted (edited) into one work about 300 years later in 200 B.C. (Morris, 1976, p. 23; McDowell, 1999, p. 406).

It is becoming increasingly popular to believe this theory. For example, some time ago I received an e-mail "informing" me that "the documentary theory is accepted by almost all scholarly interpreters." Numerous Bible commentaries, religious journals, and Web sites promote it. And many professors who teach religious courses espouse it. Undoubtedly, it is champion among topics discussed in classes on a critical introduction to the Bible. In most "scholarly" circles, if one does not hold to the Documentary Hypothesis (or at least some form of it), he is considered fanatical and uneducated. In his book, *The Darwin Wars*, Andrew Brown mentioned an interview he had with the rabbi Jonathan Sacks, in which Dr. Sacks defended the proposition that Moses wrote (or dictated) the first five books of the Bible. Brown's response was: "That is the most shocking thing I have ever heard an intellectual say" (1999, p. 167).

Why are people today having such a difficult time believing that Moses wrote the Pentateuch? Likely, the principal reason is because students are bombarded with adamant "assurance" statements like the following:

> "One of the **certain results** of modern Bible study has been the discovery that the first five books of the Old Testament were not written by Moses" (Gottwald, 1959, p. 103, emp. added).

"**It is obvious** that the Book of Genesis was not written by a single author" (Rendtorff, 1998, 14[1]:44, emp. added).

"The most determined biblicist can see that **there is no way** Moses could have written the Torah" (McKinsey, 1995, p. 366, emp. added).

Statements such as these have made their way into thousands of classrooms. Sadly, before hearing the skeptics and liberal scholars present their arguments for such beliefs, students frequently become so spellbound by the "intellectual" façade and bold affirmations of certainty that they rarely even consider the evidence at hand.

MOSES AND THE ART OF WRITING

Amazingly, one of the first assumptions upon which this theory rests was disproved long ago. From the earliest period of the development of the Documentary Hypothesis, it was assumed that Moses lived in an age prior to the knowledge of writing. One of the "founding fathers" of this theory, Julius Wellhausen, was convinced that "[a]ncient Israel was certainly not without God-given bases for ordering of human life; **only they were not fixed in writing**" (1885, p. 393, emp. added). Just a few years later, Hermann Schultz declared: "Of the legendary character of the pre-Mosaic narrators, the time of which they treat is a sufficient proof. **It was a time prior to all knowledge of writing**" (1898, pp. 25-26, emp. added). One year later, T.K. Cheyne's *Encyclopedia Biblica* was published, in which he contended that the Pentateuch was not written until **almost a thousand years after Moses** (1899, 2:2055). These suppositions most certainly had an impact on these men's belief in (and promotion of) the theory that Moses could not have written the first five books of the Old Testament.

One major problem with the Documentary Hypothesis is that we now know Moses did not live "prior to all knowledge of writing." In fact, he lived **long after** the art of writing was already known. A veritable plethora of archaeological discoveries has proven one of the earliest assumptions of the Wellhausen theory to be wrong.

- In 1949, C.F.A. Schaeffer "found a tablet at Ras Shamra containing the thirty letters of the Ugaritic alphabet in their proper order. It was discovered that the sequence of the Ugaritic alphabet was the same as modern Hebrew, revealing that **the Hebrew alphabet goes back at least 3,500 years**" (Jackson, 1982, p. 32, emp. added).

- In 1933, J.L. Starkey, who had studied under famed archaeologist W.M.F. Petrie, excavated the city of Lachish, which had figured prominently in Joshua's conquest of Canaan (Joshua 10). Among other things, he unearthed a pottery water pitcher "inscribed with a dedication in eleven archaic letters, the earliest 'Hebrew' inscription known" (Wiseman, 1974, p. 705). According to Charles Pfeiffer, "The Old, or palaeo-Hebrew script is the form of writing which is similar to that used by the Phoenicians. A royal inscription of King Shaphatball of Gebal (Byblos) in this alphabet dates from about 1600 B.C." (1966, p. 33).

- In 1901-1902, the Code of Hammurabi was discovered at the ancient site of Susa (in what is now Iran) by a French archaeological expedition under the direction of Jacques de Morgan. It was written on a piece of black diorite nearly eight feet high, and contained 282 sections. In their book, *Archaeology and Bible History*, Joseph Free and Howard Vos stated:

> The **Code of Hammurabi was written several hundred years before the time of Moses** (c. 1500-1400 B.C.).... **This code, from the period 2000-1700 B.C.**, contains advanced laws similar to those in the Mosaic laws.... In view of this archaeological

> evidence, the destructive critic can no lon-
> ger insist that the laws of Moses are too
> advanced for his time (1992, pp. 103,55,
> emp. added).

The Code of Hammurabi established beyond doubt that writing was known hundreds of years before Moses.

As early as 1938, respected archaeologist William F. Albright,
in discussing the various writing systems that existed in the
Middle East during pre-Mosaic times, wrote:

> In this connection it may be said that writing was well
> known in Palestine and Syria throughout the Patri-
> archal Age (Middle Bronze, 2100-1500 B.C.). No
> fewer than five scripts are known to have been in use:
> (1) Egyptian hieroglyphs, used for personal and place
> names by the Canaanites; (2) Accadian Cuneiform;
> (3) the hieroglyphiform syllabary of Phoenicia; (4)
> the linear alphabet of Sinai; and (5) the cuneiform
> alphabet of Ugarit which was discovered in 1929 (1938,
> p. 186, parenthetical comment in orig.).

The truth is, numerous archaeological discoveries of the
past 100 years have proved once and for all that the art of writing was known not only during Moses' day, but also long before Moses came on the scene. Although skeptics, liberal theologians, and college professors continue to perpetuate the
Documentary Hypothesis, they must be informed (or reminded)
of the fact that **one of the foundational assumptions upon
which the theory rests has been completely shattered
by archeological evidence**.

EVIDENCE FOR THE DOCUMENTARY
HYPOTHESIS–REFUTED

Many of the questions surrounding this theory were answered
years ago by the respected scholar J.W. McGarvey. His book
titled *The Authorship of Deuteronomy* (first published in 1902)
silenced many supporters of the Documentary Hypothesis.

Critics simply could not overcome his ability to detect and expose the many perversions of their teachings. Over the last century, however, critics eventually regained their confidence and began citing even more "evidence" for their theory. One category of "proof" frequently mentioned by skeptics and liberal scholars is that of chronological lapses (also called anachronisms). Allegedly, numerous references found in the Pentateuch are said to be of a later time; hence, it is impossible for them to be Mosaic. According to Israel Finkelstein and Neil Silberman in their extremely popular book on archaeology and the Bible, *The Bible Unearthed*, "archaeology has provided enough evidence to support a new contention that the historical core of the Pentateuch…was substantially shaped in the seventh century BCE" (2001, p. 14; BCE stands for Before the Common Era)–about 800 years **after** Moses lived. Two years earlier, Stephen Van Eck wrote in *The Skeptical Review*: "[T]he best evidence against the Mosaic authorship is contained in the Pentateuch itself," which "contains anachronistic references impossible to be the work of Moses" (1999, p. 2). Thus, allegedly, "at the very least, we can conclude that many elements in the patriarchal narratives are unhistorical" (Tobin, 2000).

Just what are these "anachronistic references" that are "impossible to be the work of Moses"? And are there reasonable explanations for them being in the Pentateuch? What can be said about the alleged chronological lapses that have led many to believe the stories of the Bible are unhistorical?

No King in Israel...Yet (Genesis 36:31)

For most people, the 36th chapter of Genesis is "unfamiliar territory." It is known more for being the chapter **after** Genesis 35 (in which details are given about Jacob's name being changed to Israel) and **before** chapter 37 (where one can read about Joseph's brothers selling him into slavery). Nowhere does Genesis 36 record the names of such patriarchs as Abraham, Isaac, or Joseph. (And Jacob is mentioned only once.)

Nor are there any memorable stories from this portion of Genesis–of the kind that we learned in our youth. Perhaps the least-studied chapter in the first book of the Bible is Genesis 36–the genealogy of Esau.

Surprisingly, to some, this often-overlooked chapter contains one of the more controversial phrases in the book. Genesis 36:31 states: "Now these were the kings who reigned in the land of Edom, **before any king reigned over the children of Israel**" (emp. added). According to skeptics and liberal theologians, the notation "before any king reigned over the children of Israel" points to the days of the monarchs. Dennis McKinsey declared in his book, *Biblical Errancy*: "This passage could only have been written after the first king began to reign…. It had to have been written after Saul became king, while Moses, the alleged author, lived long before Saul" (2000, p. 521). Paul Tobin also indicated that this portion of the Bible "must therefore have been written, at the very earliest, after the first Jewish King, Saul, began to rule over the Israelites which was around three centuries after the death of Moses" (2000). Tobin went on to ask (what he feels certain cannot be answered): "Now how could Moses have known that there would be kings that reigned over the Israelites?"

There are two logical reasons why Moses could mention future Israelite kingship. First, Moses knew about the express promises God had made both to Abraham and Jacob concerning the future kings of Israel. On one occasion, God informed Abraham and Sarah that many kings would be among their posterity. He promised Abraham saying, "And I will bless her [Sarah–EL] and also give you a son by her: then I will bless her, and she shall be a mother of nations; **kings of peoples shall be from her**" (Genesis 17:16, emp. added). Years later (and just one chapter before the verse in question), when God appeared to Jacob at Bethel and changed his name to Israel, He said: "I am God Almighty. Be fruitful and multiply; a nation and a company of nations shall proceed from you, and **kings shall come from your body**" (Genesis 35:11, emp. added). The fact that Genesis 36:31 reads, "Now these were the kings who reigned in the land of Edom, **before any king reigned over the children of Israel**," does not mean this account must have been written by someone who lived after the monarchy was introduced to Israel. Rather, this statement was written with the **promise** in mind that kings would come out of the loins of Abraham and Jacob, and merely conveys the notion that Edom became a kingdom at an earlier time than Israel. Keil and Delitzsch remarked: "Such a thought was by no means inappropriate to the Mosaic age. For the idea, that Israel was destined to grow into a kingdom with monarchs of his [Jacob's—EL] own family, was a hope handed down to the age of Moses, which the long residence in Egypt was well adapted to foster" (1996). Furthermore, the placement of this parenthetical clause ("before any king reigned over the children of Israel") in 36:31

> was exceedingly natural on the part of the sacred historian, who, having but a few verses before (Gen 35:11) put on record the divine promise to Jacob that "kings should come out of his loins," was led to remark [discuss—EL] the national prosperity and regal establishment of the Edomites long before the organization of a similar order of things in Israel. He could not help indulging such a reflection, when he contrasted the posterity of Esau with those of Jacob from the stand point of the promise (Gen 25:23) [Jamieson, et al., 1997].

A second reason Moses is justified in having knowledge of Israelite kingship before it was known experientially is because Moses was inspired (John 5:46; Mark 12:26; cf. Exodus 20:1; 2 Timothy 3:16-17; 2 Peter 1:20-21). For someone to say that the author of Genesis could not have been Moses because the author spoke generally of Israelite kings prior to their existence, totally ignores the fact that Moses received special revelation from Heaven. Nowhere is this seen more clearly than in Deuteronomy 17:14-15. Here Moses prophetically stated:

> When you come to the land which the Lord your God is giving you, and possess it and dwell in it, and say, "I will set a king over me like all the nations that are around me," **you shall surely set a king over you whom the Lord your God chooses**; one from among your brethren you shall set as king over you; you may not set a foreigner over you, who is not your brother (emp. added).

Under normal circumstances, such foreknowledge would be impossible. One must keep in mind, however, that "with God all things are possible" (Matthew 19:26)—and God was with Moses (cf. Exodus 3:12; 6:2; 25:22).

Were the Christian to claim that Moses wrote Genesis without being inspired or without having knowledge of the earlier promises made to Abraham and Jacob about the future kingship of Israel, the critic would be correct in concluding that Genesis 36:31 is anachronistic. But, the truth is, a Christian's faith is based on the fact the Bible writers possessed access to supernatural revelation. Thus, Moses' superior knowledge is not a problem. Rather, it is to be expected.

Camels Bearing a Heavy Load (Genesis 12:16; 24:63)

Arguably, the most widely alleged anachronisms used in support of the idea that Moses could not have written the first five books of the Bible are the accounts of the early patriarchs possessing camels. The word "camel(s)" appears twenty-three times in twenty-one verses in the book of Genesis. The first book of the Bible declares that camels existed in Egypt during the time of Abraham (12:14-17), in Palestine in the days Isaac (24:63), in Padan Aram while Jacob was working for Laban (30:43), and were owned by the Midianites during the time

Joseph was sold into Egyptian slavery (37:25,36). Make no mistake about it—the book of beginnings clearly teaches that camels were domesticated since at least the time of Abraham.

According to skeptics and a growing number of "biblical scholars," however, the idea that Moses would have written about camels being domesticated in the time of Abraham directly contradicts archaeological evidence. Over one hundred years ago, Cheyne wrote: "The assertion that the ancient Egyptians knew of the camel is unfounded" (1899, 1:634). In Norman Gottwald's defense of the Documentary Hypothesis, he cited the mention of camels in Genesis as one of the main "indications that the standpoint of the writer was later than the age of Moses" (1959, p. 104). More recently, Finkelstein and Silberman confidently asserted:

> We now know through archaeological research that **camels were not domesticated as beasts of burden earlier than the late second millennium** and were not widely used in that capacity in the ancient Near East until well after 1000 BCE (2001, p. 37, emp. added).

By way of summary, what the Bible believer has been told is: "[T]ame camels were simply unknown during Abraham's time" (Tobin, 2000).

While these claims have been made repeatedly over the last century, the truth of the matter is that skeptics and liberal theologians are unable to cite one piece of solid archaeological evidence in support of their claims. As Randall Younker of Andrews University stated in March 2000 while delivering a speech in the Dominican Republic: "Clearly, scholars who have denied the presence of domesticated camels in the 2nd millennium BC have been committing the fallacy of arguing from silence. This approach should not be allowed to cast doubt upon the veracity of any historical document, let alone Scripture" (2000). The burden of proof actually should be upon skeptics to show that camels were not domesticated until after the time of the patriarchs. Instead, they assure their listeners of the camel's absence in Abraham's day without one shred of archaeological evidence. [Remember, for many years they also argued that writing was unknown during the time of Moses—a conclusion based entirely on "silence." Now, however, they have recanted that idea, because evidence has been found to the contrary.]

What makes their claims even more disturbing is that several pieces of evidence do exist (and have existed for some time) that prove camels were domesticated during (and even before) the time of Abraham (roughly 2,000 B.C.). In an article that appeared in the *Journal of Near Eastern Studies* a half-century ago, professor Joseph Free listed several instances of Egyptian archaeological finds supporting the domestication of camels. [NOTE: The dates given for the Egyptian dynasties are from Clayton, 2001, pp. 14-68]. The earliest evidence comes from a pottery camel's head and a terra cotta tablet with men riding on and leading camels. According to Free, these are both from predynastic Egypt (1944, pp. 189-190), which according to Clayton is roughly before 3150 B.C. Free also lists three clay camel heads and a limestone vessel in the form of a camel lying down—all dated at the First Dynasty of Egypt (3050-2890 B.C.). He then mentions several models of camels from the Fourth Dynasty (2613-2498 B.C.), and a petroglyph depicting a camel and a man dated at the Sixth Dynasty (2345-2184 B.C.). Such evidence has led one respected Egyptologist to conclude that "the extant evidence clearly indicates that the domestic camel was known [in Egypt—EL] by 3,000 B.C." —long before Abraham's time (Kitchen, 1980, 1:228).

Perhaps the most convincing find in support of the early domestication of camels in Egypt is a rope made of camel's hair found in the Fayum (an oasis area southwest of modern-day Cairo). The two-strand twist of hair, measuring a little over three feet long, was found in the late 1920s, and was sent to the Natural History Museum, where it was analyzed and compared to the hair of several different animals. After much testing, it was determined to be camel hair, dated (by analyzing the layer in which it was found) to the Third or Fourth Egyptian Dynasty (2686-2498 B.C.). In his article, Free also listed several other discoveries from around 2,000 B.C. and later, each of which showed camels as domestic animals (pp. 189-190).

While prolific in Egypt, finds relating to the domestication of camels are not limited to the African continent. In his book, *Ancient Orient and the Old Testament*, Kenneth Kitchen, professor emeritus of the University of Liverpool, reported several discoveries **made outside of Egypt**, proving ancient camel domestication existed around 2,000 B.C. Lexical lists from Mesopotamia have been uncovered that show a knowledge of domesticated camels as far back as that time. Camel bones have been found in household ruins at Mari in present-day Syria that fossilologists believe are also at least 4,000 years old. Furthermore, a Sumerian text from the time of Abraham has been discovered in the ancient city of Nippur (located in what is now southeastern Iraq) that clearly implies the domestication of camels by its allusions to camels' milk (Kitchen, 1966, p. 79).

All of these documented finds support the domestication of camels in Egypt many years before the time of Abraham. Yet, as Younker so well said, skeptics refuse to acknowledge any of this evidence.

> It is interesting to note how, once an idea gets into the literature, it can become entrenched in conventional scholarly thinking. I remember doing research on the ancient site of Hama in Syria. As I was reading through the excavation reports (published in French), I came across a reference to a figurine from the 2nd millennium which the excavator thought must

be a horse, but the strange hump in the middle of its back made one think of a camel. I looked at the photograph and the figurine was obviously that of a camel! The scholar was so influenced by the idea that camels were not used until the 1st millennium, that when he found a figurine of one in the second millennium, he felt compelled to call it a horse! This is a classic example of circular reasoning (2000, parenthetical comment in orig.).

Finds relating to the domestication of camels are not as prevalent in the second millennium B.C. as they are in the first millennium. This does not make the skeptics' case any stronger, however. Just because camels were not as widely used during Abraham's time as they were later, does not mean that they were entirely undomesticated. As Free commented:

Many who have rejected this reference to Abraham's camels seem to have assumed something which the text does not state. **It should be carefully noted that the biblical reference does not necessarily indicate that the camel was common in Egypt at that time,** nor does it evidence that the Egyptians had made any great progress in the breeding and domestication of camels. It merely says that Abraham had camels (1944, p. 191, emp. added).

Similarly, Younker noted:

This is not to say that domesticated camels were abundant and widely used everywhere in the ancient Near East in the early second millennium. However, the patriarchal narratives do not necessarily require large numbers of camels.... The smaller amount of evidence for domestic camels in the late third and early second millennium B.C., especially in Palestine, is in accordance with this more restricted use (1997, 42:52).

Even without the above-mentioned archaeological finds (which to the unbiased examiner prove that camels were domesticated in the time of Abraham), it only seems reasonable to conclude that since wild camels have been known since the Creation, "there is no credible reason why such an indispensable animal in desert and semi-arid lands should not have been sporadically domesticated in patriarchal times and even earlier" (see "Animal Kingdom," 1988). The truth is, all of the available evidence points to one conclusion–the limited use of domesticated camels during and before the time of Abraham. The supposed "anachronism" of domesticated camels during the time of the patriarchs is, in fact, an actual historical reference to the use of these animals at that time. Those who reject this conclusion cannot give one piece of solid archaeological evidence on their behalf. They simply argue from the "silence" of archaeology…which is silent no more!

Moses' Knowledge of Gates (Deuteronomy 15:22)

A further "proof" against Mosaic authorship is the mention of gates throughout the Pentateuch. As McKinsey wrote: "Deut. 15:22 says, 'Thou shalt eat it within thy gates.' The phrase 'within thy gates' occurs in the Pentateuch about twenty-five times and refers to the gates of Palestinian cities, which the Israelites did not inhabit until **after** the death of Moses" (1995, p. 363, emp. in orig.). In making this statement, however, Mr. McKinsey is in gross error by assuming that the passage is referring to the "gates of Palestinian cities." Moreover, what skeptics like McKinsey fail to mention is the fact that "gate" does not necessarily mean the large doors in the walls of fortified cities. Sometimes, gates are used to represent entrances into areas of dwelling, as in Exodus 32:26: "Then Moses stood **in the gate of the camp**, and said, 'Whoso is on Jehovah's side, (let him come) unto me.' And all the sons of Levi gathered themselves together unto him" (ASV, emp. added). Would anyone suppose that the Israelites built walls and gates around their Bedouin-style tent cities? Therefore, "gate" can mean the entrance to a city—of tents. In fact, the Hebrew word for gate (ša'ar) is translated as "entrance" ten times in the NIV. And in the NKJV, ša'ar is translated as "entrance" in Exodus 32:36.

Giving Dennis McKinsey the benefit of the doubt (that the term "gates" refers to the Palestinian cities) Moses could have been referring to the cities that the Israelites would capture in the future. Since he was inspired while writing the Pentateuch (cf. 2 Timothy 3:16-17; 2 Peter 1:20-21), this knowledge could have been the result of that inspiration, similar to the knowledge that Israel would one day have a king. Either way, the mention of "gates" in the Pentateuch is not anachronistic.

Dan in the Days of Abraham (Genesis 14:14)

According to Genesis 14, certain kings of the east traveled to the land of Canaan, pillaged the cities of Sodom and Gomorrah, and captured Lot, the nephew of Abraham. The Genesis record states that Abraham pursued these abductors "as far as Dan" (Genesis 14:14; cf. Deuteronomy 34:1). Many writers claim that this city was not named "Dan" until the time of the judges (Judges 18:29), and thus this section of the book of Genesis could not have been written by Moses. Allegedly, there was no place known as Dan until years after Moses lived. In fact, "Dan was built after the death of Samson, who died 350 years after the death of Moses" (McKinsey, 1995, p. 364). John Willis, in his commentary on Genesis, added: "[T]he date of the present final form of the book of Genesis cannot be earlier than that time [period of the Judges—EL], although the events that it relates and the oral or written sources from which it was composed are much earlier" (Willis, 1984, p. 229). Is such a charge correct? Does the mention of the city of Dan so early in history mean that we have a mistake in the first book of the Bible?

As is the case with many alleged discrepancies in the Bible, there are several ways of resolving this alleged difficulty. [In an article that appeared in the May 1989 issue of *Reason & Revelation*, the monthly journal on Christian evidences published by Apologetics Press, Wayne Jackson mentioned the following three (pp. 18-19).] First, it is possible that the name was given by inspiration in anticipation of later historical developments (Thornton, 1887; Judges 18:29). Although this view is not popular with most scholars, who can absolutely prove that it is incorrect? Must supernatural revelation always be eliminated from the divine record? Second, it may be that the name "Dan" was actually in use at the time of Abraham, but that it later was called Laish by the Sidonians, into whose hands it fell (Judges 18). Subsequently, it is suggested, in the time of the judges it received its original name again (Jacobus, 1864, 1:253). A third possibility is that there was another "Dan"—different from Laish Dan—(possibly referred to in 2 Samuel 24:6 and 1 Kings 15:20; cf. 2 Chronicles 16:4), which was situated near the sources of the Jordan. This location of Dan was recognized by Josephus in *The Antiquities of the Jews* (Book 1, Chapter 10, Section 1), and according to Eusebius was situated four miles west of Paneas (see Jamieson, et al., 1997). It is, therefore, "in the highest degree probable that the Dan mentioned in Genesis 14:14 was a Phoenician town already existing in the time of Abraham, or at least in the Mosaic age" (Harman, 1878, p. 160).

Canaanites were in the Land...Then (Genesis 12:6; 13:7)

Have you ever wondered why, if Moses wrote the Pentateuch, in Genesis 12:6 and 13:7 the Bible says (in reference to the time of Abraham), "[t]he Canaanites were **then** in the land" (emp. added)? If the Canaanites occupied the land of Canaan in Moses' day, why would Moses write that they were in the land **then** (i.e., in the days of Abraham)? Would these verses not make more sense if we understood them as being written

at a time when the Canaanites had been driven out of the land
of Canaan (something that would not occur until hundreds
of years **after** the death of Moses)? According to several critics, this is exactly what the verses are implying (cf. Gottwald,
1959, p. 104; McKinsey, 1995, pp. 361-362). Supposedly, Moses could not have been the author of the passage; else it would
not have made sense to its original audience.

The phrase "the Canaanites were **then** in the land" does
not necessarily have to point to a time after Moses when the
Canaanites were no longer in Canaan. When one takes the
context of these passages into consideration, and the momen-
tous events of Abraham leaving his homeland and coming to
the new region that his descendants would one day occupy,
he or she easily can understand that the phrase in question refers to this land promise (12:7). The words "then in the land"
merely are indicating "that the land into which Abram had
come was not uninhabited and without a possessor; so that
Abram could not regard it at once as his own and proceed to
take possession of it, but could only wander in it in faith as in
a foreign land (Heb. 11:9)" [Keil and Delitzsch, 1996]. Likely,
the Canaanites are mentioned as being in the land at the time
of Abraham's entrance in order "to show the strength of his
faith in the promise recorded" (Jamieson, et al., 1997). Such
phraseology involves neither a contradiction nor an absurd-
ity.

Philistines in the Time of Abraham–Fallacy or Fact? (Genesis 21:32; 26:1)

The Bible declares that long before King David fought the
Philistine giant named Goliath in the valley of Elah (1 Samuel
17), Abraham and Isaac had occasional contact with a people
known as the Philistines. In fact, seven of the eight times that
the Philistines are mentioned in Genesis, they are discussed
in connection with either Abraham's visit with Abimelech,
king of the Philistines (21:32,34), or with Isaac's visit to the

same city (Gerar) a few years later (26:1,8,14-15,18). For some time now, critics of the Mosaic authorship of the Pentateuch have considered the mention of the Philistines–so early in human history–to be inappropriately inserted into the patriarchal account. Supposedly, "Philistines...did not come into Palestine until **after** the time of Moses" (Gottwald, 1959, p. 104, emp. added), and any mention of them before that time represents "an historical inaccuracy" (Frank, 1964, p. 323). Thus, as Millar Burrows concluded, the mention of Philistines in Genesis may be considered "a convenient and harmless anachronism," which "is undoubtedly a mistake" (1941, p. 277).

As with most allegations brought against the Scriptures, those who claim the Philistine nation was not around in Abraham's day are basing their conclusion on at least one unprovable assumption–namely, that the Philistines living in the days of the patriarchs were a great nation, similar to the one living during the time of the United Kingdom. The evidence suggests, however, that this assumption is wrong. The Bible does not present the Philistines of Abraham's day as the same mighty Philistine nation that would arise hundreds of years later. Abimelech, the king of Gerar, is portrayed as being intimidated by Abraham (cf. Genesis 21:25). Surely, had the Philistine people been a great nation in the time of the patriarchs, they would not have been afraid of one man (Abraham) and a few hundred servants (cf. Genesis 14:14). Furthermore, of the five great Philistine city-states that were so prominent throughout the period of the Judges and the United Kingdom (Ashdod, Ashkelon, Ekron, Gath, and Gaza–Joshua 13:3; 1 Samuel 6:17), none was mentioned. Rather, only a small village known as Gerar was named. To assume that the Bible presents the entire civilization of the Philistines as being present during Abraham's day is to err. In reality, one reads only of a small Philistine kingdom.

The word "Philistine" was a rather generic term meaning "sea people." No doubt, some of the Aegean sea people made their way to Palestine long before a later migration took place –one that was considerably larger. In commenting on these Philistines, Larry Richards observed:

> While there is general agreement that massive set-
> tlement of the coast of Canaan by sea peoples from
> Crete took place around 1200 B.C., there is no reason
> to suppose Philistine settlements did not exist long
> before this time. In Abram's time as in the time of
> Moses a variety of peoples had settled in Canaan, in-
> cluding Hittites from the far north. Certainly the sea-
> going peoples who traded the Mediterranean had es-
> tablished colonies along the shores of the entire basin
> for centuries prior to Abraham's time. There is no
> reason to suppose that Philistines, whose forefathers
> came from Crete, were not among them (1993, p. 40).

No archaeological evidence exists that denies various groups of "sea people" were in Canaan long before the arrival of the main body in the early twelfth century B.C. (see Unger, 1954, p. 91; Archer, 1964, p. 266; Harrison, 1963, p. 32). To assume that not a single group of Philistines lived in Palestine during the time of Abraham because archaeology has not documented them until about 1190 B.C. is to argue from negative evidence, and is without substantial weight. In response to those who would deny the Philistines' existence based upon their silence in the archeological world before this time, professor Kitchen stated: "Inscriptionally, we know so little about the Aegean peoples as compared with those of the rest of the Ancient Near East in the second millennium B.C., that it is premature to deny outright the possible existence of Philistines in the Aegean area before 1200 B.C." (1966, p. 80n). Likely, successive waves of sea peoples from the Aegean Sea migrated to Canaan, even as early as Abraham's time, and continued coming until the massive movement in the twelfth century B.C. (Archer, 1970, 127:18).

Based on past experiences, one might think that critics of the Bible's inerrancy would refrain from making accusations when arguing from silence. For years, modernists and skeptics taught that the Hittite kingdom, which is mentioned over forty times in Scripture (Exodus 23:28; Joshua 1:4; et al.), was a figment of the Bible writers' imaginations, since no evidence of the Hittites' existence had been located. But those utterances vanished into thin air when, in 1906, the Hittite capital was discovered, along with more than 10,000 clay tablets that contained the Hittites' law system. Critics of the Bible's claim of divine inspiration at one time also accused Luke of gross inaccuracy because he used the title *politarchas* to denote the city officials of Thessalonica (Acts 17:6,8), rather than the more common terms *strateegoi* (magistrates) and *exousiais* (authorities). To support their accusations, they pointed out that the term politarch is found nowhere else in all of Greek literature as an official title. Once again, these charges eventually were dropped, based on the fact that the term politarchas has now been found in 32 inscriptions from the second century B.C. to the third century A.D. (Bruce, 1988, p. 324n), with at least five of these inscriptions being from Thessalonica–the very city about which Luke wrote in Acts 17 (Robertson, 1997).

Although critics accuse biblical writers of revealing erroneous information, their allegations continue to evaporate with the passing of time and the compilation of evidence. Those who reject the idea that Moses wrote the Pentateuch, and espouse the JEDP theory, do so without sufficient proof to verify their claims. As Kitchen noted: "...even the most ardent advocate of the documentary theory must admit that we have as yet **no single scrap** of external, objective (**i.e., tangible**) evidence for either the existence or the history of 'J', 'E', or any other alleged source-document" (1966, p. 23, emp. in orig.).

DOES IT REALLY MATTER WHO WROTE THE PENTATEUCH?

To some, the question of whether or not Moses wrote the first five books of the Bible is a trivial matter—one of secondary importance. After all, we do not consider it a necessity to know whom God inspired to write the book of Job or the epistle of Hebrews. We do not draw lines of fellowship over who wrote 1 and 2 Kings and 1 and 2 Chronicles. Why, then, should the discussion of who penned the first five books of the Bible be any different? **The difference is that the Bible is replete with references attributing these books to Moses**. Within the Pentateuch itself, one can read numerous times how Moses wrote the law of God.

> "Then the Lord said to Moses, 'Write this for a memorial in the book and recount it in the hearing of Joshua' " (Exodus 17:14).

> "And Moses wrote all the words of the Lord" (Exodus 24:4).

> "Then the Lord said to Moses, 'Write these words…' " (Exodus 34:27).

> "Now Moses wrote down the starting points of their journeys at the command of the Lord" (Numbers 33:2).

> "So Moses wrote this law and delivered it to the priests…" (Deuteronomy 31:9).

Bible writers throughout the Old Testament credited Moses with writing the Pentateuch. A plain statement of this commonly held conviction is expressed in Joshua 8:32: "There in the presence of the Israelites, Joshua copied on stones **the law of Moses, which he** [Moses—EL] **had written**" (NIV, emp. added). Notice also that 2 Chronicles 34:14 states: "Hilkiah the priest found **the Book** of the Law of the Lord **given by Moses**" (emp. added; cf. Ezra 3:2; 6:18; Nehemiah 13:1; Malachi 4:4). As Josh McDowell noted in his book, *More Evi-*

dence that Demands a Verdict, these verses "refer to an actual written 'law of Moses,' not simply an oral tradition" (1975, pp. 93-94).

[NOTE: The Hebrew Bible was not divided like our modern-day English Old Testament. It consisted of three divisions: the Law, the Prophets, and the Writings (cf. Luke 24:44). It contained the same "books" we have today; it was just divided differently. Genesis through Deuteronomy was considered one unit, and thus frequently was called "the Law" or "the Book" (2 Chronicles 25:4; cf. Mark 12:26). Even a casual perusal of its individual components will confirm that each book presupposes the one that precedes it. Without Genesis, Exodus reads like a book begun midway; without Exodus, Leviticus is a mystery; and so on. They were not intended to be five separate volumes in a common category, but rather, are five divisions of the same book. Hence, the singular references: "the Law" or "the Book."]

The New Testament writers also showed no hesitation in affirming that Moses wrote the Pentateuch. John wrote: "The law was given through Moses" (John 1:17). Luke recorded of the resurrected Jesus: "And beginning at Moses and all the Prophets, He expounded to them [His disciples—EL] in all the Scriptures the things concerning Himself" (Luke 24:27). Referring to the Jewish practice of publicly reading the Law, James affirmed Mosaic authorship: "For Moses has had throughout many generations those who preach him in every city, being read in the synagogues every Sabbath" (Acts 15:21). With this Paul concurred, saying, "For **Moses writes** about the righteousness which is of the law, 'The man who does those things shall live by them' " (Romans 10:5, emp. added; cf. Leviticus 18:5). In 2 Corinthians 3:15, Paul also wrote: "Moses is read." The phrase "Moses is read" is a clear example of the figure of speech known as metonymy (when authors are put for the works which they have produced) [see Dungan, 1888, pp. 273-275]. Today, we may ask someone if he has read Homer, Virgil, or Shake-

speare, by which we mean to ask if he has read the writings of
these men. In the story of the rich man and Lazarus, one can
read where Abraham spoke to the rich man concerning his
five brothers saying, "They have Moses and the prophets; let
them hear them" (Luke 16:29). Were Moses and the Old Testament prophets still on Earth in the first century? No. The
meaning is that the rich man's brothers had **the writings of
Moses** and the prophets.

Furthermore, both Jesus' disciples and His enemies recognized and accepted the books of Moses. After Philip was called
to follow Jesus, he found his brother Nathanael and said: "We
have found Him of whom **Moses in the law,** and also the
prophets, **wrote**–Jesus of Nazareth, the son of Joseph" (John
1:45, emp. added). Notice also that New Testament Sadducees considered Moses as the author, saying, "Teacher, **Moses wrote to us** that if a man's brother dies, and leaves his
wife behind, and leaves no children, his brother should take
his wife and raise up offspring for his brother" (Mark 12:19,
emp. added; cf. Deuteronomy 25:5; Luke 20:28).

A final reason that one must defend the Mosaic authorship
of the Pentateuch, instead of sitting idly by claiming, "it doesn't
really matter who wrote it," is because Jesus Himself claimed
"the Law" came from Moses. In Mark 7:10 Jesus quoted from
both Exodus 20 and 21, attributing the words to Moses. Mark
also recorded a conversation Jesus had with the Pharisees regarding what "Moses permitted" and "wrote" in Deuteronomy chapter 24 (Mark 10:3-5; cf. Matthew 19:8). Later, we
read where Jesus asked the Sadducees, "Have you not read
in the book of Moses, in the burning bush passage, how **God
spoke to him**, saying, 'I am the God of Abraham, the God of
Isaac, and the God of Jacob'?" (Mark 12:26, emp. added). But,
perhaps the most convincing passage of all is found in John 5:
46-47 where Jesus said: "For if you believed **Moses**, you would
believe Me; for he **wrote about Me**. But if you do not believe

his writings, how will you believe My words?" (emp. added; cf. Deuteronomy 18:15-18). The truth is, by claiming that Moses did not write the books of the Pentateuch, one essentially is claiming that Jesus was mistaken. M.R. DeHaan expounded upon this problem in his book *Genesis and Evolution*:

> Prove that Moses did not write the books of the Pentateuch and you prove that Jesus was totally mistaken and not the infallible Son of God he claimed to be. Upon your faith in Moses as the writer of the five books attributed to him rests also your faith in Jesus as the Son of God. You cannot believe in Jesus Christ without believing what Moses wrote. You see, there is much more involved in denying the books of Moses than most people suppose (1978, p. 41).

Indeed, believing Moses wrote the Pentateuch is very important. It is not a trivial subject we should treat frivolously while suggesting that "it really doesn't matter." It matters because the deity of Christ and the integrity of the Bible writers are at stake!

Chapter 4

ALLEGED NUMERICAL CONTRADICTIONS

HOW MANY DAUGHTERS DID LOT HAVE?
Genesis 19:8,14-16

In the famous narrative of the destruction of Sodom and Gomorrah recorded in Genesis 19, one discovers that Lot, his wife, and two daughters are led outside of the city in order to avoid death by means of fire and brimstone. Although Lot's wife was not destroyed in the devastation of these cities, she never made it to the mountains to take refuge with Lot and her daughters, but instead was turned into a pillar of salt for looking back upon the devastated cities after specifically being warned otherwise (cf. 19:17,26). Of the inhabitants of the cities who were destroyed on that day of reckoning, only Lot and his two daughters survived (19:25-26).

A casual reading of this memorable event has lead some to believe (and advocate) that there is a contradiction involving the number of Lot's daughters. In the beginning of Genesis 19, we find where Lot tells a harassing mob outside his house in Sodom that he has **"two daughters who have not known a man"** (19:8). Later, after two angels warned Lot to leave the city because it was going to be destroyed, the text says that "Lot went out and spoke to his **sons-in-law, who had married his daughters**" (19:14). The next morning the angels urged Lot to hasten their departure saying, "Arise, take your wife and your **two daughters who are here**, lest you be consumed in the punishment of the city" (19:15). While the patriarch lingered, the angels "took hold of his hand, his wife's hand, and **the hands of his two daughters**...and they brought him out and set him outside the city" (19:16).

The question that has been posed about the Bible's description of Lot's family is as follows: If Lot only had two daughters who were virgins ("not known a man"–19:8), then how could he have "sons-in-law"? Is this a legitimate contradiction, or is there an adequate explanation?

One possible explanation to this supposed contradiction is that Lot actually had **more** than two daughters. But how can that be when the text simply speaks of Lot "and his **two** daughters?" The answer could be found in verse 15, where Lot's two daughters **in the house** (19:15) might be contrasted with other daughters who were married to his sons-in-law (19: 14), and thus were **out of the house**. Since the angels who urged Lot to hasten his departure modified "two daughters" with the phrase "who are here," then it is conceivable that Lot could have had daughters elsewhere who remained in Sodom and were destroyed along with Lot's sons-in-law.

Another explanation revolves around the modifying phrase "who had married his daughters" (19:14). The words "who had married" are from the Hebrew word *laqach*, which means in the widest variety of applications "to take" or "to grasp." In this passage, the word obviously is used in reference to "taking" a wife. According to Hebrew scholar Victor Hamilton, "The Hebrew form used here is a participle (*loqcheey*), and as such is without a specific tense reference. Even the ancient versions differed on how to render the participle, with the [Latin]

Vulgate opting for a future tense, and the LXX [Septuagint—the first Greek translation of the Old Testament] opting for a past tense" (1995, p. 40, bracketed items added). Biblical commentator John Willis agreed, saying, "The Hebrew lying behind the phrase **who were to marry** can be interpreted equally well in either of two ways" (1984, p. 266). Interestingly, most modern translations (including the NAS, RSV, and NIV) agree with first-century Jewish historian Flavius Josephus in making these men **future** sons-in-law (Book 1, Chapter 11, Section 4). This is in contrast to the KJV, ASV, and NKJV, each of which renders these men as **already being** sons-in-law ("who had married"). No doubt the translators of the more modern versions believed that Lot's "sons-in-law" were only **betrothed,** not married, to Lot's daughters at the time they departed Sodom.

Other information that adds credence to the "future sons-in-law" position revolves around how people in ancient times viewed their future spouses. In the first chapter of the first book in the New Testament, we read where Joseph was called Mary's "husband" while they were betrothed and before they were married. The text reads:

> After His [Jesus'—EL] mother Mary was **betrothed** to Joseph, **before they came together,** she was found with child of the Holy Spirit. Then **Joseph her husband,** being a just man, and not wanting to make her a public example, was minded **to put her away** secretly. But while he thought about these things, behold, an angel of the Lord appeared to him in a dream, saying, "Joseph, son of David, do not be afraid **to take to you Mary your wife,** for that which is conceived in her is of the Holy Spirit" (Matthew 1:18-20, emp. added).

The wording of this passage is not just a simple use of "prolepsis" (the assignment of a name, description, or event to a time that precedes it). Rather, betrothal was a valid marriage in Jewish law (see Jamieson, et al., 1997). When marriage vows were said at the betrothal, a "putting away" or a divorce was required to end them. Furthermore, according to Josephus' comments about Hyrcanus II being Herod's father-in-law four years before Herod married his daughter (Mariamne), **espousals of old were a sufficient foundation for kinship** (Book 14, Chapter 3, Section 1).

In light of all this information, one obviously can understand that there is no contradiction in Genesis 19. Either Lot had more than two daughters (which the text allows), or Lot's two virgin daughters were betrothed to men who were called Lot's sons-in-law before the marriage was consummated. It is my judgment that, in view of the evidence, the latter is the more likely explanation. But, regardless of which explanation is correct, we may rest assured that no contradiction exists.

HOW MANY SUPERVISORS DID SOLOMON HAVE?
1 Kings 5:16; 2 Chronicles 2:18

A helpful concept to remember when one is dealing with alleged discrepancies is the idea (discussed in chapter one) that a simple difference is not necessarily a contradiction. Just because two texts differ in the way they relate the facts, does not necessarily mean that there exists no possible reconciliation of the texts. Notice an example of texts that differ, yet do not contradict each other.

> 1 Kings 5:16: "Besides Solomon's chief officers that were over the work, **three thousand and three hundred**, who bare rule over the people that wrought in the work."

> 2 Chronicles 2:18: "And he set threescore and ten thousand of them to bear burdens, and fourscore thousand that were hewers in the mountains, and **three thousand and six hundred** overseers to set the people at work."

These two verses often have been accused of contradicting one another because 1 Kings mentions 3,300 supervisors over the people, while 2 Chronicles mentions 3,600 overseers. However, to label these passages as contradictory represents a misunderstanding that could be based on several factors. One possible solution to this alleged contradiction is that the author of 2 Chronicles could be including a number of reserves who were standing ready to work, should any of the "regular" supervisors get sick or accidentally be killed.

Respected Old Testament commentators, Keil and Delitzsch, offered another solution. They pointed out the fact that 1 Kings 9:23 mentions 550 chief officers of Solomon, thus giving the total number of supervisors in 1 Kings 5:16 and 9:23 as 3,850. Also mentioned is the fact that 2 Chronicles 8:10 mentions 250 chief officers of Solomon, bringing the total number of officers in 2 Chronicles 2:18 and 8:10 to exactly 3,850–the same total as in 1 Kings. The difference then does not lie within the numbers of the text; rather, it seems **the two authors may have simply classified the officers according to different standards**. Whereas the chronicler might have been dividing the supervisors according to their nationality, the author of 1 Kings seems to have been dividing them by their authority (1996).

HOW MUCH WATER COULD "THE SEA" HOLD?
1 Kings 7:26; 2 Chronicles 4:5

Almost 1,000 years before Jesus set foot on the Earth, the first temple dedicated to Jehovah was built out of Lebanon cedar (which was considered the finest wood available), costly stones, and pure gold. The Bible indicates that over 183,000 men were involved in the construction of this glorious house of worship during the reign of King Solomon (1 Kings 5:13-16). The vessels that were housed within the temple, and those that remained in the inner court, were equally as elaborate. One of these vessels that stood on the right side of the sanctuary between the altar and the porch of the temple was an immense bronze basin known as "the Sea" (1 Kings 7:23). It was five cubits (7½ feet) high, ten cubits (15 feet) in diameter at the brim, thirty cubits (45 feet) in circumference and rested on 12 bronze oxen (1 Kings 7:23-26, 39; 2 Chronicles 4:2-5,10). Unlike the ten lesser basins that were used to bathe portions of the burnt offerings, the Sea served as a washing pool for the priests (2 Chronicles 4:6). For many years the capacity of the inner court's large basin known as "the Sea" has been at the center of controversy. The reason: 1 Kings 7:26 indicates that it held 2,000 baths (a bath was the largest of the liquid measures in Hebrew culture; comparative estimates range from 4.5-9 U.S. gallons). However, 2 Chronicles 4:5 says that the Sea held 3,000 baths. Thus, critics of the Bible's inerrancy have charged that a blatant contradiction exists and that such lack of agreement discredits divine authorship.

There are at least three possible solutions to this alleged contradiction. First, the answer could be that a copyist, while attempting to ensure a "carbon copy" of the manuscript from which he was working, made an error. [See chapter seven for more information on copyists' errors.] Keil and Delitzsch, in their commentary on 2 Chronicles, indicated their support of this theory. They tend to believe that the number 3,000 given in 2 Chronicles 4:25 has arisen from the confusion of ג (Hebrew letter-number for 3) with ב (Hebrew letter-number for 2). By a comparison of the two Hebrew letters, it is easy to see that their shape is quite similar. Even a tiny smudge from excessive wear on a scroll-column or a slightly damaged manuscript could have resulted in making the Hebrew letter number for 3 (ג) look like the Hebrew letter number for 2 (ב). With such an adjustment, the statements in 1 Kings and 2 Chronicles are harmonized easily. However, it very well may be that this is not a copyist's error at all.

A second possible explanation to this alleged contradiction revolves around a Hebrew word used in 2 Chronicles 4:5 that does not appear in 1 Kings 7:26. Whereas in 1 Kings it says that the molten Sea "held" (ASV) 2,000 baths, 2 Chronicles says that it "**received** (Hebrew *mach°ziyq*) **and held** three thousand baths" (ASV, emp. added). The difference in phraseology may indicate that the Sea ordinarily contained 2,000 baths, but when filled to its utmost capacity it received and held 3,000 baths (Haley, 1951, p. 382). Thus, the chronicler informs the reader that 3,000 baths of water were required to completely fill the Sea, which usually held 2,000 baths (Barnes, 1997). Anyone who has ever been around large pools of water (like a swimming pool) knows that the pool actually can hold a few thousand gallons of water more than generally is kept in it. It very well may be that the wording in 2 Chronicles indicates such a difference about the water level in the Sea.

A third possible solution to this "problem passage" is that the "bath" unit mentioned in 1 Kings was larger than the "bath" unit used in 2 Chronicles. Since the latter account was written after the Babylonian exile, it is quite possible that reference is made to the Babylonian bath, which might have been less than the Jewish bath used at the time of Solomon. As Adam Clarke observed: "The cubit of Moses, or of the ancient Hebrews, was longer than the Babylonian by one palm.... It might be the same with the measures of capacity; so that two thousand of the ancient Jewish baths might have been equal to three thousand of those used after the captivity" (1996). In considering modern-day examples, a 20% difference exists between the U.S. gallon and the Imperial gallon, even though the same term is used for both quantities. Also, the furlong of London in 1475 was 625 feet, while the furlong of the same city in 1600 was 660 feet (cf. Revelation 14:20). Thus, the alleged discrepancy between 1 Kings 7:26 and 2 Chronicles 4:5 may be simply a misunderstanding on the part of twenty-first-century readers.

The fact of the matter is that critics of the Bible cannot prove that this is a legitimate contradiction. Second Chronicles could represent a copyist's error. On the other hand, I believe that one of the last two explanations represents a more plausible solution to the problem: either (1) the addition of the Hebrew word *mach°ziyq* ("received") in 2 Chronicles 4:5 means that the Sea could actually hold 3,000 baths (though it normally held 2,000 baths); or (2) the "bath" unit used during the time of Solomon was larger than the one used after the Jews were released from Babylonian captivity. Until one proves that these three solutions are not possibilities, he should refrain from criticizing the Bible's claim of divine inspiration.

3 OR 3.14?
1 Kings 7:23-26

The dimensions of Solomon's Sea also have been a problem to some. Not only has the capacity been challenged, but also its circumference. We read that the container was circular, being 10 cubits in diameter and having a circumference of 30 cubits. Now, a basic rule of math is that the circumference should equal the diameter multiplied by pi (which is approximately 3.14). However, if we work the opposite way and divide 30 by 10, we get a value of exactly 3. This apparent discrepancy is used by many critics to show that the Bible is not inerrant, and therefore, not divinely inspired.

One common explanation is that the diameter was measured from the outside walls of the vessel, while the circumference was measured on the inside walls. This gives a thickness for the walls of 8 to 9 inches. However, 1 Kings 7:26 states that the walls were a "handbreadth thick." A handbreadth is an ancient unit of measure equal to about 3 inches, which makes this solution inadequate.

A better response may be just to recognize that Scripture does not speak of measurements with the scientific accuracy of our modern age. There was no specific standard by which

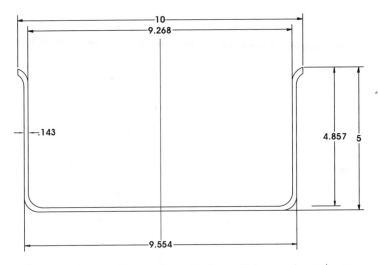

Diagram showing dimensions of Solomon's bronze basin (units in cubits). Based on A. Zuidhof (1982), "King Solomon's Molten Sea and (π)," *Biblical Archaeologist*, 45:179-184.

to measure things in Bible times. For example, the ancients relied upon the size of a person's hands to measure the "span" of an object. In order to determine the length of larger things, people would use the distance from their elbow to the end of their middle finger, which was considered a cubit. These measurements obviously were not intended to be as precise as things measured in the twenty-first century–everyone's hands and forearms were not the same size. The small difference between 3 and 3.14, then, should not cause a problem for sincere Bible students. Sadly, hard-headed skeptics will argue that the resulting error of a ½ to 1½ cubits (depending on the dimensions being measured) is unacceptable in a book that is supposed to be inerrant.

Interestingly, the recorded dimensions are still no problem if we consider the shape of the vessel. In 1 Kings 7:26, we read that its "brim was made like the brim of a cup, as a lily blossom." Hence, the Sea was not a regular cylinder, but had an outward curving rim. Although we do not know the exact points on the vessel where the measurements were taken, the main part of the Sea always will be somewhat smaller than the 10 cubits measured "from brim to brim." Indeed, if we divide the recorded circumference by the accepted value of pi, we arrive at a main diameter of 9.554 cubits (see figure on previous page). It is easy to imagine some ancient inspector simply measuring across the top of the basin, then measuring its girth, and not giving one thought to the false accusations of unbelievers 3,000 years away.

COCK-A-DOODLE-DO...TWICE?
Matthew 26:34; Mark 14:30; Luke 22:34; John 13:38

Perhaps the most famous alleged Bible contradiction centers on Peter's triple denial of Jesus and the crowing of a rooster. For years, skeptics have charged that Mark's account of this event blatantly contradicts the other gospel accounts, thus supposedly "proving" the imperfection of the Scriptures. Even Bible believers have questioned the differences surrounding this event, yet relatively few have taken the time to understand them. Whenever people ask us about Peter's denials and the differences within the gospel accounts, we often fail to give an adequate answer to their questions (cf. 1 Peter 3:15). This lack of understanding and poor defense of God's Word has led skeptics to become more confident in their position (that the Bible is not God's Word), and has caused some Bible believers to abandon their position on the infallibility of the Scriptures.

The passages in question are found in Matthew 26, Mark 14, Luke 22, and John 13. Matthew, Luke, and John all quoted Jesus as saying that Peter would deny Him three times before the **rooster crowed**.

> Jesus said to him, "Assuredly, I say to you that this night, before the rooster crows, you will deny Me three times" (Matthew 26:34).

> Then He said, "I tell you, Peter, the rooster shall not crow this day before you will deny three times that you know Me" (Luke 22:34).

> Jesus answered him… "Most assuredly, I say to you, the rooster shall not crow till you have denied Me three times" (John 13:38).

After the third denial actually took place, these three writers recorded that Jesus' prophecy was fulfilled exactly the way He said it would be.

> And immediately a rooster crowed. And Peter remembered the word of Jesus who had said to him, "Before the rooster crows, you will deny Me three times" (Matthew 26:74b-75).

> Immediately, while he was still speaking, the rooster crowed. And the Lord turned and looked at Peter. And Peter remembered the word of the Lord, how He had said to him, "Before the rooster crows, you will deny Me three times" (Luke 22:60-61).

> Peter then denied again [for the third time—EL]; and immediately a rooster crowed (John 18:27).

Matthew, Luke, and John all indicated that Peter denied Jesus three times before the rooster crowed. Mark's account, however, says otherwise. He recorded Jesus' prophecy as follows: "Assuredly, I say to you that today, even this night, before the rooster crows **twice**, you will deny Me three times" (Mark 14:30, emp. added). Following Peter's first denial of Jesus, we learn that he "went out on the porch, and a rooster crowed" (Mark 14:68). After Peter's third denial of Jesus, the rooster crowed "a second time…. Then Peter called to mind the word that Jesus had said to him, 'Before the rooster crows twice, you will deny Me three times' " (Mark 14:72).

Mark differs from the other writers in that he specifies the rooster crowed once after Peter's first denial and again after his third denial. But do these differences represent a legitimate contradiction? Do they indicate, as some critics charge, that the Bible is not from God? Absolutely not!

Consider the following illustration. A family of three went to a high school football game together for the first time. The father and son had been to several games prior to this one, but the mother never had been fortunate enough to attend a high school football game until now. After entering the stadium, Jack tells his 16-year-old son, Chris, that they will meet him just outside Gate 12 immediately after **the** buzzer sounds. Having filed the instructions away, Chris races to the stands to ensure that he sees the opening kickoff. Jack's wife, Tammy, who did not hear the instructions he gave Chris, then asks him when they were going to see Chris again. He responds, "We are going to meet him just outside the gate we just entered after the **fourth** buzzer." After the fourth buzzer? But he told Chris after **the** buzzer sounded they would meet him. Did Jack contradict himself? No. At this particular stadium, the time keepers normally sound a buzzer after each quarter. But, when we say "at the buzzer" or when we speak of "a buzzer beater," usually we are referring to the final buzzer. Chris was familiar with sports lingo, and thus Jack told him he would see him "after the buzzer sounds." Tammy, on the other hand, having never attended a football game in her life, was given different instructions. In a more precise way, Jack instructed her that Chris would meet them, not after the first, second, or third buzzer, but after the fourth and final buzzer that marks the end of regulation. Jack knew that if he told Tammy, "Chris will meet us after the buzzer sounds," she would expect to meet him after the first buzzer sounded. Thus, Jack simply informed Tammy in a more detailed manner. Surely no one would claim that Jack contradicted himself.

In a similar way, no one should assume that because three of the gospel writers mentioned one crowing, while Mark mentioned two crowings, that a contradiction exists. In actuality, there were two "rooster crowings." However, it was the second one (the only one Matthew, Luke, and John mentioned) that was the "main" crowing (like the fourth buzzer was the "main" buzzer at the football game). In the first century, roosters were accustomed to crowing at least twice during the night. The first crowing (which only Mark mentioned—14:68) usually occurred between twelve and one o'clock. Relatively few people ever heard or acknowledged this crowing (see "cock," *Fausset's Bible Dictionary*). Likely, Peter never heard it; else surely his slumbering conscience would have awakened.

The second crowing took place not long before daybreak. It was this latter crowing that was commonly called "the cockcrowing." Why? Because it was at this time of night (just before daybreak) that roosters crowed the loudest, and their "shrill clarion" was useful in summoning laborers to work (see "cockcrowing," McClintock and Strong, 1968, 2:398). This crowing of the roosters served as an alarm clock to the ancient world. Mark recorded earlier in his gospel account that Jesus spoke of this "main" crowing when He stated: "Watch therefore, for you do not know when the master of the house is coming—in the evening, at midnight, **at the crowing of the rooster**, or in the morning" (Mark 13:35, emp. added). Interestingly, even when workers were called to work via artificial devices (e.g., bugles), this time of the night still was designated by the proverbial phrase, "the cockcrowing." If you lived in the first century and your boss said to be ready to work when "the rooster crows," you would know he meant that work begins just before daybreak. If he said work begins at the second crowing of the rooster, likewise, you would know he meant the same thing—work begins just before daylight. These are not contradictory statements, but two ways of saying the same thing.

When Jesus said, "Before the rooster crows, you will deny Me three times" (Matthew 26:34), He was using "the rooster crows" in the more conventional way. Mark, on the other hand, specified that there were two crowings. In the same way that the husband tells his wife more detailed instructions concerning a football game, Mark used greater precision in recording this event. It may be that Mark quoted the exact words of Jesus, while the other writers (under the guidance of the Holy Spirit) saw fit to employ the less definite style to indicate the same time of night (McGarvey, 1875, p. 355). Or, perhaps Jesus made both statements. After Peter declared that he never would deny the Lord, Jesus could have repeated His first statement and added another detail, saying: "[E]ven this night, before the rooster crows **twice**, you will deny Me three times" (Mark 14:30, emp. added). We cannot be sure why Mark's account is worded differently than the other writers, but by understanding that "the rooster crowing" commonly was used to indicate a time just before daybreak, we can be assured that no contradiction exists among the gospel writers.

HOW MANY THIEVES REVILED CHRIST?
Matthew 27:44; Mark 15:32; Luke 23:39

Very likely, the most well-known, nameless person in the Bible is "the thief on the cross." The Lord demonstrated His mercy one last time before His crucifixion by pardoning the thief who begged Jesus, saying, "Lord, remember me when You come into Your kingdom" (Luke 23:42). Having the "power on Earth to forgive sins" (Matthew 9:6), and an overflowing amount of compassion, Jesus told him: "Assuredly, I say to you, today you will be with Me in Paradise" (Luke 23:43).

After rehearsing the story of "the thief on the cross" countless times from Luke's gospel account, some Bible students are puzzled when they eventually compare the "beloved physician's" account with what Matthew and Mark recorded. Whereas Luke wrote: "Then **one** of the criminals who were hanged blasphemed Him, saying, 'If you are the Christ, save Yourself and us' " (23:39), Matthew and Mark stated the following:

> "Even **the robbers** who were crucified with Him reviled Him" (Matthew 27:44).

> "Even **those** who were crucified with Him reviled Him" (Mark 15:32).

The obvious question is, why did Matthew and Mark indicate the "thieves" (plural) reviled Jesus, while Luke mentioned only one who insulted Him?

First, it is quite possible that, initially, both thieves reviled Christ, but then one of them repented. After hearing Jesus' words on the cross, and seeing His forgiving attitude, the one thief may have been driven to acknowledge that Jesus was indeed the Messiah. How many times have we made a statement about someone or something, but then retracted the statement only a short while later after receiving more information?

A second possible explanation for the minor differences in gospel accounts regarding the two thieves who were crucified next to Jesus involves the understanding of a figure of speech known as synecdoche. Merriam-Webster defines this term as "a figure of speech by which a part is put for the whole (as *fifty sail* for *fifty ships*), the whole for a part (as *society* for *high society*)...or the name of the material for the thing made (as *boards* for *stage*)" (italics in orig.). Just as Bible writers frequently used figures of speech such as simile, metaphor, sarcasm, and metonymy, they also used synecdoche. As seen above (in the definition of synecdoche), this figure of speech can be used in a variety of ways (see also Dungan, 1888, pp. 300-309):

- A whole can be put for the part.
- A part may be put for the whole.
- Time might be put for part of a time.
- The singular can be put for the plural.
- And the plural can be put for the singular.

It is feasible that Matthew and Mark were using the plural in place of the singular in their accounts of the thieves reviling Christ on the cross. Lest you think that such might be an isolated case, notice two other places in Scripture where the same form of synecdoche is used.

> Genesis 8:4 indicates that Noah's ark rested on "on the **mountains** of Ararat." Question: Did the ark rest on one of the mountains of Ararat, or did it rest on all of them at the same time? Although the ark was a huge vessel, it obviously did not rest on the many mountains of Ararat; rather, it rested on one.

> In Genesis 21:7 Sarah asked, "Who would have said to Abraham that Sarah would nurse **children**? For I have borne him a son in his old age." Anyone who knows much about the Bible will remember that Sarah had but **one** child. In certain contexts, however, one might use synecdoche and speak of one child (as did Sarah) by using the word children.

We must keep in mind that the biblical apologist does not have to pin down the exact solution to an alleged contradiction; he need show only one or more possibilities of harmonization in order to negate the force of the charge that a Bible contradictions really exists. The skeptic cannot deny that both of the above options are plausible explanations to the question of why Matthew and Mark wrote of "thieves" reviling Christ, instead of "thief."

23,000 OR 24,000?
1 Corinthians 10:8; Numbers 25:9

In 1 Corinthians 10:7-10, the apostle Paul gave four "examples" of how God's chosen people in the Old Testament sinned by lusting "after evil things." At one time or another, the Israelites had been guilty of worshipping false gods (vs. 7), committing sexual immorality (vs. 8), as well as tempting God and complaining against the Almighty (vss. 9-10). It is the second example Paul provided in this list (involving the Israelites' sexual immorality) that has been the brunt of much criticism. Allegedly, this verse is in direct opposition with what Moses recorded in the Pentateuch. Whereas Paul stated, "[I]n one day twenty-three thousand [Israelites–EL] fell" as a result of their sexual immorality (1 Corinthians 10:8), Moses recorded that "those who died in the plague were twenty-four thousand" (Numbers 25:9).

Some apologists (Archer, 1982, p. 401; Geisler and Howe, 1992, pp. 458-459) have attempted to resolve this infamous case of "the missing thousand" by claiming that the Old Testament event to which Paul alluded was the plague Jehovah sent upon the people after they made a golden calf (Exodus 32:35), and not the plague recorded in Numbers 25:9. The problem with this explanation is that the Israelites' sin in Exodus 32 was idolatry, not the sexual immorality of which Paul says that the 23,000 were guilty (1 Corinthians 10:8). Although idolatry sometimes included sexual immorality, most likely Paul was not referring to the events that took place after Moses' descent from Mount Sinai (Exodus 32).

So how can we explain Paul's statement in light of the information given in Numbers 25:9 (the probable "sister" passage to 1 Corinthians 10:8)? The answer lies in the fact that Paul stated 23,000 fell **"in one day,"** while in Numbers 25 Moses wrote that the **total number** of those who died in the plague was 24,000. Moses never indicated how long it took for the 24,000 to die; rather, he only stated that this was the number "who died in the plague." Thus, the record in 1 Corinthians simply supplies us with more knowledge about what occurred in Numbers 25—23,000 of the 24,000 who died in the plague died "in one day."

It is very troubling to see how some other apologists attempt to explain this alleged contradiction. In their popular book *Hard Sayings of the Bible*, Walter Kaiser, Peter Davids, Manfred

Brauch, and F.F. Bruce made the following comments regarding "the missing thousand" in 1 Corinthians 10:8:

> It is possible that Paul, citing the Old Testament from memory as he wrote to the Corinthians, referred to the incident in Numbers 25:9, but **his mind slipped** a chapter later in picking up the number.... [W]e cannot rule out the possibility that there was some reference to 23 or 23,000 in his local environment as he was writing and that caused **a slip in his mind** (1996, p. 598, emp. added).

> Paul was not attempting to instruct people on Old Testament history and certainly not on the details of Old Testament history (p. 598).

> Thus here we have a case in which **Paul apparently makes a slip of the mind** for some reason (unless he has special revelation he does not inform us about), but the mental error does not affect the teaching. How often have we heard preachers with written Bibles before them make similar errors of details that in no way affected their message? If we notice it (and few usually do), we (hopefully) simply smile and focus on the real point being made. As noted above, Paul probably did not have a written Bible to check (although at times he apparently had access to scrolls of the Old Testament), but in the full swing of dictation **he cited an example from memory and got a detail wrong** (pp. 598-599, parenthetical comments in orig., emp. added).

Supposedly, Paul just made a mistake. He messed up, just like when a preacher today mistakenly misquotes a passage of Scripture. According to the repetitious testimony of these men, Paul merely had "a slip of the mind" (experiencing what some today might call a "senior moment"), and our reaction (as well as the skeptics') should be to "simply smile and focus on the real point being made."

Unbelievable! These men pen an 800-page book in an attempt to answer numerous alleged Bible contradictions and to defend the integrity of the Bible, and they have the audacity to say that the apostle Paul "cited an example from memory and got a detail wrong." Why in the world did they spend so much time (and space) answering the numerous questions that skeptics often raise, and then conclude that the man who penned almost half of the New Testament books made mistakes in his writings?! They have concluded exactly what the infidel teaches—Bible writers made mistakes. Furthermore, if Paul made one mistake in his writings, he easily could have blundered elsewhere. And if Paul made mistakes in other writings, how can we say that Peter, John, Isaiah, and others did not "slip up" occasionally? The fact is, if Paul or any of these men made mistakes in their writings, then they were not inspired by God (cf. 2 Timothy 3:16-17; 2 Peter 1:20-21), for God does not make mistakes (cf. Titus 1:2; Psalm 139:1-6). And if the Scriptures were not "given by inspiration of God," then the Bible is not from God. And if the Bible is not from God, then the skeptic is right. But as we noted above, the skeptic is not right! First Corinthians 10:8 can be explained logically— without assuming that Paul's writings are inaccurate.

Sadly, Kaiser, et al., totally dismiss the numerous places where Paul claimed his writings were from God. When Paul wrote to the churches of Galatia, he told them that his teachings came to him "through revelation of Jesus Christ" (1:12). In his first letter to the Thessalonian church, he claimed that the words he wrote were "by the word of the Lord" (4:15). To the church at Ephesus, Paul wrote that God's message was "revealed by the Spirit to His holy apostles and prophets" (3:5). In 2 Peter 3:16, Peter put Paul's letters on a par with the Old Testament Scriptures when he compared them to "the rest of the Scriptures." And in the same epistle where Kaiser, et al., claim Paul "makes a slip of the mind," Paul said, "the things which I write to you are the commandments of the Lord" (1 Corinthians 14:37).

Paul did not invent facts about Old Testament stories. Neither did he have to rely on his own cognizance to remember particular numbers or names. The Holy Spirit revealed the Truth to him–**all** of it (cf. John 14:26; 16:13). Just like the writers of the Old Testament, Paul was fully inspired by the Holy Spirit (cf. 2 Samuel 23:2; Acts 1:16; 2 Peter 1:20-21; 3:15-16; 2 Timothy 3:16-17). When he wrote to the Corinthians about the 23,000 Israelites who fell in one day as a result of their sexual immorality, we can be certain that he reported the account correctly.

THE "TWELVE"

1 Corinthians 15:5; Matthew 27:5; Acts 1:15-26

Numerous alleged Bible discrepancies arise because skeptics frequently interpret figurative language in a literal fashion. They treat God's Word as if it were a dissertation on the Pythagorean theorem, rather than a book written using ordinary language. They fail to recognize the inspired writers' use of sarcasm, hyperbole, prolepsis, irony, etc. Such is the case in their interpretation of 1 Corinthians 15:5. Since Paul stated that "the twelve" (apostles) saw Jesus after His resurrection, these critics claim that Paul clearly erred because there were not "twelve" apostles after Jesus' resurrection and before His ascension. There actually were only eleven apostles during that time. [Judas already had committed suicide (Matthew 27:5), and Matthias was not chosen as an apostle until after Jesus' ascension into heaven (Acts 1:15-26).] Skeptics claim Paul's use of the term "twelve" when speaking about "eleven" clearly shows that the Bible was not "given by inspiration of God."

The simple solution to this numbering "problem" is that "the twelve" to which Paul referred was not a literal number, but the designation of an office. This term is used merely "to point out the society of the apostles, who, though at this time they were only eleven, were still called the twelve, because this was their original number, and a number which was afterward filled up" (Clarke, 1996). Gordon Fee stated that Paul's use of the term "twelve" in 1 Corinthians 15:4 "is a clear indication that in the early going this was a **title** given to the special group of twelve whom Jesus called to 'be with him' (Mark 3:14). Thus this is their collective designation; it does not imply that all twelve were on hand, since the evidence indicates otherwise" (1987, p. 729, emp. added).

This figurative use of numbers is just as common in English vernacular as it was in the ancient languages. In collegiate sports, one can read about the Big Ten conference, which consists of eleven teams, or the Atlantic Ten conference, which is made up of twelve teams. At one time these conferences only had ten teams, but when they exceeded ten teams, they kept their original conference "names." Their names are a designation for a particular conference, not a literal number. In 1884, the term "two-by-four" was coined to refer to a piece of lumber two-by-four inches. Interestingly, a two-by-four is still called a two-by-four, even when it is trimmed to slightly smaller dimensions (1 5/8 by 3 5/8). Again, the numbers are more of a designation than a literal number.

Critics like Steve Wells, author of the *Skeptic's Annotated Bible*, misrepresent the text when they claim Paul taught: "Jesus was seen by **all** twelve apostles (**including Judas**) after Judas' suicide and before Jesus' ascension" (emp. added). Paul did not teach that Jesus was seen by **all** twelve of the **original** apostles (including Judas). The text simply says Jesus "was seen by Cephas, then by the twelve." As already noted, skeptics reject the explanation that Paul used the term "twelve" in a figurative sense (yet they must admit that such numbers can be, and frequently are, used in such a way). These critics also disregard the possibility that "the twelve" may have included Matthias, the apostle who took Judas' place (Acts 1:15-26). Although in my judgment Paul was using "the twelve" in a figurative sense, it is possible that he was including Matthias with "the twelve."

Matthias had been chosen as one of the apostles long before Paul wrote 1 Corinthians, and we know he was a witness of the resurrection of Christ (cf. Acts 1:21-22). In fact, it is very likely that he was part of the group that "gathered together" with the apostles when Christ appeared to them after His resurrection (cf. Luke 24:33). When Paul wrote of "the twelve," it may be that he was using a literary device known as prolepsis. Thus, no one can say for sure that Matthias was not included in "the twelve" mentioned by Paul.

Does Paul's reference to "the twelve" in 1 Corinthians 15:5 contradict Jesus' appearances to ten of the apostles on one occasion (John 20:19-23) and eleven on another (John 20:26-29)? Not at all. Either he simply used a figure of speech common to all languages—where several persons (or groups) who act as colleagues are called by a number rather than a name—or he was including Matthias.

Chapter 5

ALLEGED GEOGRAPHICAL CONTRADICTIONS

WHERE DID JOSIAH DIE?
2 Kings 23:29-30; 2 Chronicles 35:23-24

Thirty-one years after inheriting the kingdom of Judah from his father, Josiah traveled to the Valley of Megiddo and fought against Pharaoh Necho, King of Egypt. The Bible gives few details about this battle, but what it does tell us has caused some to question the Bible's accuracy. Skeptics allege that a contradiction exists between 2 Kings 23 and 2 Chronicles 35. The writer of 2 Kings recorded that "Pharaoh Necho killed him (Josiah–EL) at Megiddo when he confronted him." Then, later, "his servants moved his body in a chariot from Megiddo, brought him to Jerusalem, and buried him in his own tomb" (23:29-30). When the writer of Chronicles wrote of these events, he recorded that after King Josiah was struck with arrows, he said to his servants, "Take me away, for I am severely wounded." After that "his servants therefore took him out of that chariot and put him in the second chariot that he had, and they brought him to Jerusalem." Then the text says, "So he died, and was buried in one of the tombs of his fathers" (2 Chronicles 35: 23-24). Because the writer of 2 Kings recorded that Pharaoh Necho killed Josiah **at Megiddo**, and the chronicler used the phrase, "so he died" **after** writing that Josiah's body was returned to Jerusalem, skeptics charge that the recorded history of one or both of the writers is wrong.

If 2 Kings 23 were the only account we had of Josiah's death, then one might very well assume that he took his last breath at Megiddo. But, since 2 Chronicles 35 indicates that he was alert enough after he was shot to command his servants to take him away, we know that he did not die immediately. However, he still may have died in Megiddo after he uttered this command. Or, he could have died on the way to Jerusalem. The accounts can be reconciled even if he had died in Jerusalem. Just because 2 Kings 23:29 says that Pharaoh Necho killed Josiah at Megiddo does not have to mean that he actually died there. It easily could mean that he was mortally wounded at Megiddo, and then died sometime later. If someone today is shot in a back alley late at night, he may be rushed to the hospital in hopes that his life might be saved. However, if he dies, whether it is on the way to the hospital or in the hospital, those who rehearse the details of the shooting likely will **not** say that he "died in a hospital," but that he was "killed in the back alley."

Furthermore, just because the writer of 2 Chronicles wrote the phrase "so he died" after he mentioned that Josiah was brought to Jerusalem, does not mean that he did not die beforehand. As E.M. Zerr observed in his *Bible Commentary*: "The statement **and he died**...is just a common form of expression in the Bible, where the several facts of a circumstance may be named with very little regard for their chronological order" (1954, pp. 278-279, emp. in orig.). The acknowledgment of the chronicler that Josiah died is just that—an acknowledgment. It says nothing about **when** he died.

The facts of the story are as follows: (1) Josiah was wounded fatally at Megiddo; (2) his body was rushed away to Jerusalem after he commanded his servants to take him away; and (3) he died sometime after he gave that command. The text is not clear as to the exact location of his death. He could have passed away in Megiddo, on his way to Jerusalem, or even in Jerusalem for that matter. However, the latter is not likely to have occurred, since Jerusalem was over fifty miles from Megiddo (probably no less than a two-hour chariot ride). Neither account clearly defines the location of death, but instead states only that the location of the fatal injury occurred in Megiddo. We must remember that "where two different, but not conflicting accounts of an event are given, one more specific than the other, the one that is clearer should be used to explain the other" (Zerr, pp. 278-279).

Those who claim that these two passages are contradictory are grasping at straws. The only difference in the texts is that one is more descriptive than the other.

JESUS' SERMON ON...THE MOUNT OR THE PLAIN?

Matthew 5:1; Luke 6:17

In the introductory comments to Jesus' oft'-quoted sermon recorded in Matthew chapters 5-7, the first verse sets the stage for His "astonishing teachings." Matthew indicated that "seeing the multitudes," Jesus "went up **on a mountain**, and when He was seated His disciples came to Him." When Luke gave the setting for Jesus' masterful sermon, he stated that Jesus "came down with them and stood **on a level place**." The question that has been asked by many people is why Matthew recorded Jesus preaching this sermon from a **mountain**, while Luke said it was while He stood on **a level place**. Could Matthew or Luke have made a legitimate geographical error here, or is there a reasonable explanation for the difference that exists?

First of all, for these passages to be contradictory, one must assume that the two sermons were delivered at the same place and at the same time. But, as H. Leo Boles stated in his commentary on Luke, this sermon "may have been repeated a number of times and Luke gives a record of the sermon which was repeated at some later time than the record given by Matthew" (1940, p. 134). It certainly is possible that Jesus repeated His teachings on various occasions. He easily could have preached the beatitudes in Capernaum as well as in Cana. He could have taught the model prayer in both Bethany and Bethsaida. Who are we to say that Jesus preached the principles and commands found in Matthew 5-7 **only once**? There are some men today who travel to a different city nearly every week preaching the same sermons—and do so effectively. Could Jesus not have done something similar?

A more likely solution to this geographical "problem" is simply to understand that Matthew and Luke were referring to the same sermon, and that Jesus was preaching it while being both on a mountain and on a "plain" (KJV) at the same time. The word "plain" (*tópou pedinoú*) simply means "level place" (*Wycliffe Bible Commentary*, 1985), and is translated thusly in nearly all modern versions of the Bible. Since a mountain can have level places on it, no one can assert logically that Matthew 5:1 and Luke 6:17 are contradictory. I have been to the top of a mountain in Anchorage, Alaska, that is so level it is known as "Flattop Mountain." To say Jesus stood on a **level place** on a **mountain** is no oxymoron.

WHERE ARE YOU FROM?
Mark 1:29; John 1:44; Matthew 2:1; Acts 22:8

Although it sounds like an easy question, for a growing number of people it is becoming more and more difficult to answer: Where are you from? Ask the eighteen-year-old college freshman who grew up in a military family where she is from, and you likely will hear her rattle off five or six different states (and perhaps even a few countries!). Ask the son of a Major League baseball player (who has played for eight different teams in his twenty-year career) where he is from, and you might hear him respond by saying, "I was reared in a lot of places." Ask a preacher's kid where he was reared, and you likely will hear the same response.

It seems like the longer I live, the more problems I have telling people "where I'm from." I was born in Macon, Georgia, moved to Tennessee for five years, then back to Georgia for two, to Oklahoma for the next twelve, and then back to Tennessee (in three different cities) for the next six years. I now live in Alabama. Today, when someone asks me, "Where are you from?," I must confess that I sometimes do not know what to say. "The last move I made was from Tennessee. I spent most of my "growing-up years" in Oklahoma. I was born in Georgia...." Where am I from? Take your pick.

Some critics actually think they have a legitimate Bible contradiction on their hands by pointing out that different passages sometimes speak of the same person being from two (or more) different places. For example, in Mark 1:21-29, Simon (Peter) and his brother Andrew are said to have lived in (or very near) **Capernaum**. The apostle John, on the other hand, recorded that "the city of Andrew and Peter" was **Bethsaida** (1:44). Are these two accounts contradictory? No. Peter and Andrew were living in Capernaum at the beginning of Jesus ministry; however, they were known as being "of" Bethsaida, which is probably where they first learned a trade, got married, and made a name for themselves. The writers are simply referring to two different times in the lives of Peter and Andrew.

A similar "controversy" surrounds whence Jesus came. Well-known skeptic Dennis McKinsey had the audacity to ask, "Why would Jesus be called 'Jesus of Nazareth' when He was born in Bethlehem of Judea?" (2000, p. 133). Obviously, Mr. Mc-

Kinsey is not willing to give the Bible writers the same freedom we have today when we talk about our "hometown" and our "birthplace." The fact is, Jesus was born in Bethlehem (Matthew 2:1), but grew up in Nazareth (Matthew 2:23; cf. Acts 22:8).

Remember, for something to be a legitimate contradiction, the **same person, place, or thing** must be under consideration at the **same time** in the **same sense**. If not, then it is impossible to know that two things are contradictory.

AN INLAND "COAST"

Matthew 16:13; Mark 7:31

An unbeliever once charged the Bible with an error because the King James Version speaks of the "coasts" of Caesarea Philippi (Matthew 16:13) and the "coasts" of Decapolis (Mark 7:31). Looking at a map of the land of Palestine in the first century, a person quickly realizes that both of these regions are inland and have no coasts. So how do we explain the Bible's use of the word "coasts"?

Our modern word coast means "land along side the sea; seashore." However, in the seventeenth century when the King James Version of the Bible was translated, the term also meant "the frontier or borderland of a country." The critic's objection is based upon an obsolete usage in the KJV, and thus is not valid. In Matthew 16:13, the American Standard Version states that Jesus came into "the parts" of Caesarea Philippi. The New King James Version renders the expression as "the region." The Greek term is *ta mere*, which can denote simply a district or region (Arndt and Gingrich, 1967, p. 507).

The word rendered coasts in Mark 7:31 is the Greek *horion* (cf. English, "horizon"), and again, the meaning simply is "boundary, district, region, etc." (Arndt and Gingrich, pp. 584-585). The ASV uniformly renders it "borders," and even the KJV translates it as "borders" in Matthew 4:13. Thus, there is absolutely no biblical error involved in these passages, but merely a misunderstanding of the KJV translation.

CONTROVERSIAL JERICHO

Luke 10:30; 18:35-43; Matthew 20:29-34; Mark 10:46-52

Although the city of Jericho is mentioned only seven times in the New Testament, the passages in which the city is found have been under heavy attack by critics for centuries. Perhaps the most famous alleged geographical discrepancy surrounding Jericho is found in Luke 10 where Jesus told His unforgettable parable about the Good Samaritan. Jesus began the story saying, "A certain man went **down** from Jerusalem to Jericho" (10:30, emp. added). Many through the years have assumed Jesus was implying that Jericho was **south** of Jerusalem, since the man "went down" to get there. However, a quick look at a map of first-century Palestine (which can be found in the backs of most modern Bibles) shows that Jericho is several miles **north-east** of Jerusalem. Without looking any further into the geographical surroundings, one might assume that this represents a genuine discrepancy. After all, how can someone go "down" from point A to point B, if point B is north of point A?

As always, once all the facts are established, Jesus' statement reconciles itself with truth quite easily. Although Jericho may be several miles **north** of Jerusalem, it is more than 3,500 feet **lower** in altitude. (Jerusalem is situated at an elevation of 2,550 feet above sea level, whereas Jericho is about 1,200 feet below sea level.) There is no way for a man to journey from Jerusalem to Jericho without going **down in elevation**. Needless to say, the argument which suggests that Jesus did not know His geography has been expelled from most skeptics' repertoires in modern times. I only wish such could be said of the accusations surrounding the **miracle** He worked near the city of Jericho.

The case of the healing of the blind men near Jericho (recorded in Matthew 20:29-34, Mark 10:46-52, and Luke 18: 35-43) has been highly criticized by skeptics. While both Mark and Luke mention the healing of only **one** blind man, Matthew records the healing of **two** men as Christ made His way to Jerusalem for the final Passover. Also, Matthew and Mark indicate that the blind men were healed as Jesus was **leaving** Jericho, whereas Luke suggests that a blind man was healed as the Lord **came near** to the city. Allegedly, these differences surrounding Jesus' miracle in the city of Jericho prove the fallibility of Bible writers.

In the first place, the fact that two of the gospel accounts mention only one blind man, while the other mentions two, need not concern us. Just because Mark and Luke speak of only one blind man does not mean that they have at the same time denied that there were two blind men. Had Mark and Luke stated that Christ healed **only one man**, while Matthew then affirmed that **more than one** were healed, a contradiction would be apparent. But such is not the case. If one says, "Tim has a son," he is not contradicted if someone else says, "Tim has a son and a daughter." His statement was merely supplemented. [Matthew is the only one who recorded that Jesus performed this healing by a touch (20:34), but he does not give us the spoken words Jesus uttered, as do Mark (10: 52) and Luke (18:42).] There is no conflict, therefore, regarding the number of men involved. The accounts merely supplement one another. [This same reasoning should be used when dealing with the **two** demoniacs Matthew mentions (8: 28ff.), compared with the **one** that Mark (5:2ff.) and Luke (8: 27ff.) mention.]

Moreover, the fact that Mark mentioned by name one of the blind men (Bartimaeus), and his father (Timaeus, 10:46), might possibly indicate that Mark was centering on the blind man that he knew personally. If you lived during the time of

Jesus, and witnessed Him healing a number of people (one of whom was someone you knew), it would be understandable that when you returned home and spoke to your family, you might speak only of the friend whom Jesus healed. In no way is this being deceitful.

But how shall the second difficulty be resolved? Is there any logical reason as to why Matthew and Mark indicated that the blind men were healed as Jesus was **leaving** Jericho, while Luke mentioned that a blind man was healed as the Lord **came near** to the city? Actually, there are at least two realistic possibilities as to why the accounts are worded differently. First, it is possible that **three** blind men were healed in the vicinity of Jericho on this occasion. The instance mentioned by Luke as occurring when Jesus approached the city might have represented a different case than that recorded by Matthew and Mark. This explanation is supported by the fact that

> Luke refers only to a "multitude" of people being present as Jesus entered the city (18:36), but both Matthew (20:29) and Mark (10:46) make a point to say there was a "great multitude" of people there by the time Jesus left the city. If the word spread of the miraculous healing on the way into the city, this would account for the swelling of the crowd (Geisler and Howe, 1992, p. 353).

Though this suggestion about there being three blind men is considered by many to be remote, it is at least possible—and that is **all that is required** to negate an alleged discrepancy.

Another possible way to harmonize these passages is to understand that, during this period, there actually were two Jerichos. First, there was the Jericho of Old Testament history (Joshua 6:1ff.; 1 Kings 16:34) that was located at the sight of Elisha's spring. In the first century, however, that city existed as a small village lying mostly in ruins; about two miles south of that site was the new Jericho, built by Herod the Great. The

Lord, therefore, traveling toward Jerusalem, would first pass through the **Old Testament Jericho**, and then, some two miles to the southwest, go through **Herodian Jericho**. Accordingly, the references of Matthew and Mark to Jesus leaving Jericho would allude to old Jericho, whereas Luke's observation of Jesus drawing near to Jericho would refer to the newer city. Hence, the miracles under consideration may have been performed **between** the two Jerichos (Robertson, 1930, 1:163). Lest you think this option is incredible, consider the town of Zugres located in eastern Ukraine. Two miles from the center of this town lies the "suburb" known as Zugres 2. What are the chances that residents living in these two towns have used language similar to that used by Matthew, Mark, and Luke?

When a person studies passages such as these (which critics allege are contradictory), one important fact should be remembered: If there is **any** reasonable way of harmonizing the records, no legitimate contradiction can be charged to the accounts. Unless one can show that the same thing is under consideration at the same time and in the same sense, then it cannot be considered a legitimate contradiction. Remember, a mere difference does not a contradiction make!

GEOGRAPHY IN GENERAL

Luke 24:50-51; Acts 1:9-12

Have you ever stopped to consider how flexible people are when using geographical terms to describe somewhere they have been in the past or are going in the future? Perhaps you have heard friends telling about their trip to Dallas, Texas, to watch the Dallas Cowboys play football. The truth is, however, the Cowboys technically do not play in Dallas, Texas, but in Irving, Texas. It may be that one day your family decides to take a trip to Atlanta, Georgia, to go to Six Flags. If you do, make sure you first understand that Six Flags is not exactly in Atlanta, but in Austell, Georgia.

Oftentimes, when discussing details regarding a particular geographical region (and the towns, cities, and attractions within that region), general terms are stated in place of an exact location. A person who lives in Sand Springs, Oklahoma, often will tell people he lives in Tulsa. Why? Because Sand Springs is a suburb of Tulsa, and more people have heard of Tulsa than Sand Springs. The same is true with nearly all suburbs of major cities. Sometimes even small "country" towns are equated with their "neighbors up the road." My wife and I used to live in the small, west-Tennessee town of Clarksburg. Yet, even though we lived in Clarksburg, we had a Huntingdon, Tennessee, address—and the city of Huntingdon was ten miles away! When people asked where we lived, I said Clarksburg. When they asked for our address, I told them Huntingdon. Yet, regardless of whether I said Huntingdon or Clarksburg, no one ever accused me of lying.

Considering how much "leeway" we allow ourselves today when speaking about geographical regions, it is not surprising to find Bible writers using that same freedom in the documents they wrote for regular people (just like you and me). Although skeptics also use the same approximation that Bible writers sometimes used, they arbitrarily reject the Bible writers' information, and consider it inaccurate and uninspired. For example, in his attempt to "disprove" two biblical passages referring to the location from which Jesus ascended, skeptic Steve Wells commented: "Luke says Jesus ascended from Bethany, but Acts (1:9,12) says he ascended from Mount Olivet" (2001). As is sometimes the case with skeptics, Mr. Wells misrepresented Luke. The inspired writer of the "third" gospel account actually wrote: "And He [Jesus] led them out **as far as Bethany**, and He lifted up His hands and blessed them. Now it came to pass, while He blessed them, that **He was parted from them** and carried up into heaven" (Luke 24:50-51, emp. and bracketed note added). Notice, he did not say that

Jesus ascended "from" Bethany, but that they had gone "as far as" (*hoes pros*, literally "till over against") Bethany, and from this point Jesus ascended into heaven. The *New International Version* seems to capture the real meaning of this verse, saying that Jesus took His apostles **"in the vicinity of Bethany"** before ascending into heaven. As one can see, the text does not say that He ascended **directly** "from Bethany."

That point aside, since **Bethany was located** just one-and-three-quarter miles from Jerusalem **on the eastern slope of the Mount of Olives** (Pfeiffer, 1979, p. 197), Luke merely used different geographical referents to establish the same location—the gospel of Luke refers to the vicinity of Bethany, whereas the book of Acts mentions specifically the Mount of Olives.

THE ACCURACY OF ACTS
Acts 14:5-12

Archaeology is one of many disciplines that can be used to prove the historical accuracy of Scripture. Time and again, it has helped confirm the Bible's references to people, places, and dates. In the last one hundred years, archaeologists repeatedly have confirmed and illuminated the historicity of the Bible. Although one should not rely upon archaeology to establish and sustain his faith, having physical evidence that confirms the historical context of God's saving acts results in the sincere person's willingness to accept the Bible as God's Word.

When renowned archaeologist Sir William Ramsay started his explorations in Asia Minor, he had serious doubts about the historicity of the book of Acts. But after hundreds of hours of research, he began to change his mind. A careful study of Acts 14:5-12 led him to believe that Luke was quite familiar with the places, people, and events about which he wrote. In this passage, Luke wrote that Paul and Barnabas fled from Iconium to "Lystra and Derbe, cities of Lycaonia" (14:6). It formerly was assumed in ancient geography that Iconium was a city of Lycaonia (e.g., Montgomery is a city of Alabama).

This passage was considered by some Bible critics to be a typical example of the lack of local exactitude by the author of Acts, and thus evidence against divine inspiration. However, as Ramsay went on to demonstrate conclusively, this was not the case. Iconium was not a part of Lycaonia. Rather, it belonged to Phrygia, an entirely different district of Asia Minor. This change may sound like a minor point, but it was a very important one in the thought processes of Ramsay. His attitude toward the book of Acts began to change radically. The more he studied Acts, the more he became an ardent advocate of the trustworthiness of Luke's scholarship.

Archaeology can be a great asset to people who are searching for knowledge. It enlightens our reading of Scripture as it continues to confirm the Bible's historical accuracy. Those who have studied the book of Acts in light of archaeology have found that where references are checkable, Luke was always correct, regardless of the country, city, island, or person he mentioned. As Wayne Jackson observed: "This is truly remarkable, in view of the fact that the political/territorial situation of his day was in a state of almost constant change. **Only inspiration can account for Luke's precision**" (1991, 27[1]: 2, emp. added). How very true.

MACHPELAH OR SHECHEM?
Acts 7:15-16; Genesis 49:29-30

In Acts 7, Stephen had been accused of speaking out publicly against the temple, and of advocating the overthrow of the Law of Moses. The Sanhedrin convened to discuss his fate, and to hear his defense. At one point during his discourse, Stephen asserted: "Jacob went down to Egypt; and he died, he and our fathers. And they were carried back to Shechem and laid in the tomb that Abraham bought for a sum of money from the sons of Hamor, the father of Shechem" (7:15-16). This statement has been the brunt of much criticism because it seems to be in conflict with Genesis 49:29-30. Whereas Ste-

phen apparently stated that Jacob was buried in **Shechem**,
Genesis 49 states that Jacob was buried at **Machpelah** in Hebron, 50 miles away. Is there a legitimate explanation to this
alleged contradiction? Yes, there is.

On occasion, when the English text seems unclear or appears to contradict itself, it often is beneficial to examine the
original language in which the passage was written. This is one
such instance. A general reading of this text in a standard English translation gives one the idea that the pronoun "he" (Jacob) and the noun "fathers" are common subjects of one verb
("died"), and that the predicate phrase "were carried back to
Shechem" describes both Jacob ("he") and the "fathers." But,
in the original language the construction is different. The Greek
word rendered "died" (*eteleutasen*) is a singular verb, and can
only agree with the singular pronoun "himself." The plural
noun "fathers" is not the subject of that verb, but of the plural
verb "were carried" (*metelethasan*). Thus, the plural verb ("were
carried") belongs to "fathers," and not to Jacob. As one of the
leading biblical scholars of the late nineteenth century, J.W.
McGarvey, noted in his commentary on the book of Acts,

> The two clauses, properly punctuated, and with the
> ellipsis supplied, read thus: **"and he died; and our
> fathers *died*, and were carried over into Shech-
> em."** With this rendering and punctuation, which are
> certainly admissible, the contradiction totally disap-
> pears; and if the passage had been thus rendered at
> first into English, a contradiction would not have been
> thought of (1892, p. 121, emp. added, italics in orig.)

McGarvey's point is this: If Jacob were buried at Machpelah
in Hebron (and of that there is no doubt; cf. Genesis 49:29-30),
then Stephen must have been saying that it was the **fathers
alone** who were buried in Shechem, and not Jacob. We know
that at least one of the fathers (Joseph) was buried in Shechem
(Joshua 24:32). And while the Old Testament does not record

the burial places for many of the other patriarchs, Stephen was "full of the Holy Spirit" (7:55; cf. 6:8,10; 7:51). He had supernatural knowledge. He knew that some of the patriarchs had been buried in Shechem. Furthermore, it seems this information could have been gleaned even from secular sources. In his discussion on Acts 7, the well-known commentator Albert Barnes mentioned that some Jewish historians (e.g., Kuinoel) thought the fathers were buried at Shechem (1949, p. 124). In addition, McGarvey quotes Jerome, a fourth-century writer from Palestine, saying: "The twelve patriarchs were buried not in Arbes (Hebron), but in Shechem" (1892, p. 122).

As some might point out, however, the idea that the patriarchs were buried in Shechem was neither popular nor representative of the common Jewish thought of the day. The fact is, Josephus and other Jewish historians suggested that the fathers were buried at Hebron, not Shechem. But considering who inhabited Shechem, there is a very good reason why they would say such a thing. The Samaritans—the Jews' bitterest rivals—had seized Shechem. The proud Jews, therefore, would have done anything—perhaps even going so far as to falsify history—to keep from admitting that their ancestors were buried in their enemy's land. This actually lends credibility to Stephen's statement. Given the choice of two answers, one popular and untrue, the other true and unpopular, Stephen doubtlessly would have chosen the latter.

ALL THE WORLD IN 30 YEARS?

Colossians 1:23

According to skeptics, the apostle Paul made a factual blunder when he claimed that the Gospel had been preached to "every creature under heaven" (Colossians 1:23). If conservative scholars are correct in dating the writing of the book of Colossians around A.D. 61 (coinciding with Paul's Roman imprisonment recorded in Acts 28:30), then Paul wrote this statement only 30 years after the church was established. Could the Gospel have circled the globe in 30 years? A person living in first-century Palestine very likely would have comprehended neither the vastness of planet Earth, nor the extent to which humans had gone to inhabit it after dispersing from the Tower of Babel. There is no evidence that Paul or his fellow Christians knew anything about the ancient inhabitants of China or the Americas. Not only would their ignorance of these places hinder them from making the journey, but it also is questionable whether any first-century Christian could have journeyed to the New World. While we might be inclined to answer the difficulty by saying, "with God all things are possible," it is not necessary to invoke a miracle to understand this verse. Three observations may be helpful in clearing away the confusion that sometimes surrounds Paul's comment.

First, human communication is full of **phenomenal** language (viz., language that discusses things as they seem). Even though we "enlightened" moderns know that the Sun doesn't really rise and set (instead, the Earth turns toward and away from the Sun), we still talk about sunrise and sunset. This kind of language also occurs in the Bible (e.g., Ecclesiastes 1:5; Matthew 5:45). The Bible no more indicates that the Sun literally "rises" in the morning and "sets" in the evening than doctors believe that a pregnant woman's **water** can literally **break**. Technically, it is not correct to refer to a woman's amniotic fluid as water; nor is it correct to refer to the water as "breaking." Yet doctors frequently employ this kind of language. Surely, if modern man, with all his advanced technology, can use such phenomenal language, the Bible writers can be afforded the same luxury.

Second, biblical writers sometimes used phenomenal language in **restricted contexts**. In other words, a statement may describe something as it appears in a particular location, though not everywhere. When Jesus spoke of the kingdom of heaven and compared it to the mustard seed, which was "the least of all seeds" (Matthew 13:32), He was speaking from the vantage point of the Palestinian citizen–not that of a modern botanist. We know that it is not really the smallest of **all** seeds. No doubt Jesus knew that, too. It was the smallest seed one would plant in a Palestinian garden. Jesus was not concerned about the size of the seed in an absolute sense; He was making a common comparison from a specific context to illustrate the growth potential of the Kingdom.

Third, hyperbole (exaggeration) is a common figure of speech that does not imply dishonesty or error when intentionally employed to make a point. For example, Matthew 3:5 records that "Jerusalem, all Judea, and all the region around the Jordan" were baptized by John. A strictly literal reading of this verse would lead one to conclude that every man, woman, and child had been baptized by John. But, since Luke 20:5 implies that some of the Jewish leaders had rejected John's baptism, obviously not everyone in Judea had been baptized. The apparent conflict dissolves if we allow the possibility that Matthew was using hyperbole (something we use in English quite frequently) in his description of the far-reaching effects of John's ministry.

These three observations should help dispel the confusion over Paul's statement in Colossians 1:23. When he said the Gospel had been preached to "every creature under heaven," he was using phenomenal language to make a hyperbolic (exaggerated) claim within a specific context–namely, that the then-known world (what "appeared" to be the whole world) had heard the Gospel.

A few years earlier when Paul wrote to the Romans, he was aware that the Gospel had not yet gone to Spain (Romans 15:20-24). We have no record that he or anyone else had gone there before he wrote to the Colossians. So it seems that Paul was under no illusion regarding the extent to which the Gospel had spread. His emphasis appears to be on the great strides that had been made in such a short time (due to the faithful effort of the apostle and his colleagues) to win the world for Christ.

Chapter 6

ALLEGED CONTRADICTIONS PERTAINING TO TIME

HOW LONG WAS THE ARK OF THE COVENANT IN KIRJATH JEARIM?
1 Samuel 7:2; 2 Samuel 6:2-3; Acts 13:21

After the Philistines suffered various misfortunes for their seizure of the ark of the covenant (1 Samuel 5), the Bible indicates that they returned the ark to the Israelite city known as Kirjath Jearim. According to 1 Samuel 7:2, "the ark remained in Kirjath Jearim a long time; **it was there twenty years**. And all the house of Israel lamented after the Lord" (emp. added). The person who is familiar with Hebrew history immediately recalls, however, that the ark of God, which was sent to Kirjath Jearim before Saul's kingship began, was not retrieved from there until a few years into King David's reign. Considering Saul ruled Israel for 40 years (Acts 13:21), this passage has presented itself to some as confusing and problematic. How does the "twenty years" reference in 1 Samuel 7:2 harmonize with the fact that the ark was not brought from Kirjath Jearim until 2 Samuel 6:4—more than 40 years later?

Even though God's Word can be substantially communicated from one language to another, the translation process is sufficiently complex to the extent that many of the subtleties of the parent language are lost in translation. These subtleties rarely, if ever, involve matters that are critical to the central purpose of revelation. However, apparent discrepancies on minor details can surface that require a careful re-examination of the actual linguistic data of the parent language (in this case Hebrew) in order to dissolve the apparent contradiction.

The individual clauses of 1 Samuel 7:2-3 are linked in Hebrew by "*waw* consecutives" that bring the statements into close logical and temporal connection. The three verbs of verse two are a continuation of the infinitive, which points to the main sentence being resumed in verse three ("and Samuel spoke"). The gist of these grammatical data is that the writer is informing us that after the ark's capture, the people endured Philistine oppression for the next twenty years. Though all Israel "lamented after the Lord," He allowed the Israelites to continue their suffering at the hands of the Philistines for 20 years—at which time Samuel called upon the nation to put away its idols.

First Samuel describes the final years of the period of the judges. The reliance upon the ark as a sort of mystical talisman brought swift military tragedy, precipitating yet another period of foreign oppression by Israel's enemies due to their own apostasy. This period of Philistine preeminence went on for twenty years before the lamentations of God's people were finally heard. At the end of the twenty years, Samuel called on them to couple their lamentations with genuine penitence (1 Samuel 7:3). When they put away their idolatry (vs. 4), they once again enjoyed the services of the judge (vs. 6), who assisted them in throwing off Philistine oppression by military defeat (vss. 10ff.).

Thus the twenty years refers—not to the total number of years that the ark remained in Kirjath Jearim—but merely to the number of years the ark was in Kirjath Jearim before the Lord chose to hear the people's lamentations and provide them with intervention through Samuel.

WHEN DID BAASHA REIGN?
1 Kings 16:8; 2 Chronicles 16:1

In the book of 1 Kings, we read that Baasha became the third ruler of the Northern kingdom (Israel) "in the third year of Asa king of Judah...and reigned twenty-four years" (15:33). Then, when Baasha died, his son Elah became king over Israel "in the **twenty-sixth year of Asa**, king of Judah" (16:8, emp. added). However, 2 Chronicles 16:1 reads: "In the **thirty-sixth year of the reign of Asa**, Baasha king of Israel came up against Judah and built Ramah, that he might let none go out or come in to Asa king of Judah" (emp. added). The obvious question from anyone who reads these two passages is: How could Baasha be ruling over Israel in the thirty-sixth year of Asa's reign, when 1 Kings 16 clearly indicates that Baasha had died when Asa (the third king of the southern kingdom) was only in the twenty-sixth year of his reign? Is it possible to reconcile 1 Kings 16:8 with 2 Chronicles 15:19-16:1? Or, is this a legitimate contradiction that should lead all of us to conclude that the Bible is a worthless, man-made book of myths?

There are two possible solutions to this problem. To begin with, it may be that the numbers recorded in 2 Chronicles 15:19 and 16:1 simply are the result of a copyist's error. Although skeptics may scoff at attempts to reconcile "contradictions" by claiming a copyist must have made an error sometime in the distant past, the fact is, copyists were not infallible; inspired men were the only infallible writers. Whenever duplicates of the Old Testament Scriptures were needed, copies had to be made by hand—a meticulous, prolonged, and mentally exhausting undertaking that demanded acute awareness. History records that copyists (such as the Masoretes) had as their goal to produce accurate copies of Scripture, and that they went to great lengths to ensure fidelity in their copies. They were, nevertheless, still human. And humans are prone to make mistakes, regardless of the care they take or the strictness of the rules under which they operate. The copyists' task was made all the more difficult by the sheer complexity of the Hebrew language, and by the various ways in which potential errors could be introduced. [See chapter seven for more information on copyists' errors.]

In their commentary on 2 Chronicles, Keil and Delitzsch proposed that the number 36 in 2 Chronicles 16:1 and the number 35 in 15:19 are a scribal error for 16 and 15, respectively. The ancient Hebrew letters *yod* and *lamed*, representing the numbers 10 and 30, could have been confused and interchanged quite easily (though inadvertently) by a copyist. Merely a smudge from excessive wear on a scroll-column, or a punctured or slightly torn manuscript, could have resulted in making the ל (*yod*) look like a י (*lamed*). Furthermore, it also is possible that this error occurred first in 2 Chronicles 15:19. Then to make it consistent in 16:1, a copyist may have concluded that 16 must be an error for 36 and changed it accordingly (see Archer, 1982, p. 226). Hence the numbers 35 and 36 could have arisen out of the original 15 and 16. With such an adjustment, the statements in 1 Kings and 2 Chronicles are harmonized quite easily.

A second possibility as to why the numbers in 1 Kings 16:8 and 2 Chronicles 15:19-16:1 seem contradictory is because the numbers may refer to the thirty-fifth and thirty-sixth years **after the division of the United Kingdom** (which would have been Asa's fifteenth and sixteenth years), rather than the thirty-fifth and thirty-sixth years **of Asa's reign** (Thiele, 1951, p. 59). The Hebrew word for "reign" (*malkuwth*) also can mean "kingdom." In fact, fifty-one out of the ninety-one times this word appears in the King James Version of the Old Testament, it is translated "kingdom" (cf. 2 Chronicles 1:1; 11:17; 20:30; Nehemiah 9:35; etc.). In their commentary on 2 Chronicles, Jamieson, Faussett, and Brown favored this explanation, saying, "The best Biblical critics are agreed in considering this date to be calculated from the separation of the kingdoms, and coincident with the 16th year of Asa's reign" (1997). [The number 16 is obtained by subtracting the reigns of Rehoboam (17 years) and Abijah (3 years) from the 36 years mentioned in 2 Chronicles 16:1.] But, as Gleason Archer recognized:

> It is without parallel to refer to the kingdom of a nation as a whole and identify it thus with one particular king who comes later on in the ruling dynasty. And the fact that in its account of the later history of Judah no such usage can be instanced in Chronicles raises a formidable difficulty to this solution (1982, p. 225).

First Kings 16:8 reveals that Baasha could not have ruled over Israel in the thirty-sixth year of Asa's reign in Judah. Either the numbers 35 and 36 in 2 Chronicles 15:19-16:1 are a copyist's error, or they represent the total number of years since the United Kingdom divided. Whichever is the case, both provide possible solutions to the alleged problem that exists between the two passages. In no way should the differences that exist between 1 Kings 16:8 and 2 Chronicles 15:19-16:1 cause one to reject the Bible as God's inspired Word.

A COIN CALLED "DARIC"
1 Chronicles 29:7

Before Solomon began building the "holy house" of God, his father David challenged the Israelites to consecrate themselves by bringing an offering to the Lord that would be used in the temple's construction (1 Chronicles 29:3-5). The text says that "the leaders of the fathers' houses, leaders of the tribes of Israel, the captains of thousands and of hundreds, with the officers over the king's work, offered willingly" (29:6). They gave 5,000 talents of gold, 10,000 talents of silver, 18,000 talents of bronze, and 100,000 talents of iron. First Chronicles 29:7 also indicates that these Israelites gave 10,000 **darics** of gold.

The use of currency known as darics in a narrative that predated the invention of the currency by 500 years has led some to believe that the author of Chronicles lacked divine guidance. These critics correctly assert that the daric was a coin of the Persian Empire (probably derived from Darius the Mede). Furthermore, **it is true** that even though the chronicler used the daric to evaluate a temple offering that took place around 970 B.C., this coinage was unknown to David (*Wycliffe Bible Commentary*, 1985). It was not minted before 515 B.C. (Dillard and Longman, 1994, p. 171), and probably was not known in Palestine until the fifth century B.C. (when the book of Chronicles likely was written). So why does this **not** invalidate the inerrancy of the Scriptures? After all, a narrative that has things (like money) in it that obviously did not exist when the narrative took place is nothing but a fairy tale, is it not?

Actually, the use of the term "daric" by the writer of Chronicles in the fifth century B.C. does not mean that he believed (or wanted his readers to believe) that the Israelites in David's time possessed darics. The chronicler merely expressed—in language that would be intelligible to his readers—the sum of the gold donated by the Israelites, without intending to assume that there were darics in use in the time of David (Keil and Delitzsch, 1996). He simply used a term that was popular in his own day to help his readers better understand the sacrifice of those who gave the gold (cf. Ezra 2:69; 8:27; Nehemiah 7:70-72)—a literary device known as prolepsis.

It is possible that this is not the first time the writer of Chronicles used such conversion measures. In 2 Chronicles 4:5, the text states that the molten Sea that sat in the inner court of the temple held 3,000 baths (a bath was the largest of the liquid measures in Hebrew culture). However, 1 Kings 7:26 says that the same Sea held 2,000 baths. These numbers may be different because the "bath" unit mentioned in 1 Kings was larger than the "bath" unit used in 2 Chronicles. Since the Chronicles account was written after the Babylonian exile, it is quite possible that reference is made to the Babylonian bath, which might have been less than the Jewish bath used at the time of Solomon (Clarke, 1996).

Admittedly, the writer of Chronicles used measures of his period familiar to modern readers, even when writing about events that took place 500 years beforehand. However, converting measures does not destroy the inerrancy of Scripture!

"THREE DAYS AND THREE NIGHTS"
Matthew 12:40; 17:23; Mark 8:31; Acts 10:40

The most frequent reference to Jesus' resurrection reveals that He arose from the grave **on** the third day of His entombment. Matthew, Mark, and Luke all record Jesus as prophesying that He would rise from the grave on this day (Matthew 17:23; Mark 9:31; Luke 9:22; et al.). The apostle Paul wrote in his first epistle to the Corinthians that Jesus arose from the grave "the third day according to the Scriptures" (1 Corinthians 15:4). And while preaching to Cornelius and his household, Peter taught that God raised Jesus "**on** the third day" (Acts 10:40, emp. added). Skeptics are quick to assert, however, that these statements blatantly contradict both Matthew 12:40, wherein it is recorded that Jesus told the Pharisees He would be in the heart of the Earth "three days and three nights," and Mark 8:31, which states that Jesus would rise "**after** three days" (emp. added).

While through the eyes of the twenty-first-century reader, these statements may appear superficially to contradict one another, in reality they harmonize perfectly if one understands the liberal methods ancients used when reckoning time. In the first century, any part of a day could be computed for the whole day and the night following it (cf. Lightfoot, 1979, pp. 210-211). The Jerusalem Talmud quotes rabbi Eleazar ben Azariah, who lived around A.D. 100, as saying: "A day and night are an Onah ['a portion of time'] and the portion of an Onah is as the whole of it" (from Jerusalem Talmud: Shabbath ix. 3, as quoted in Hoehner, 1974, 131:248-249, bracketed comment in orig.). Azariah indicated that a portion of a twenty-four-hour period could be considered the same "as the whole of it." Thus, in Jesus' time, He would have been correct in teaching that His burial would last "three days and three nights," even though it was not three complete 24-hour days.

The Scriptures are filled with references which show that a part of a day sometimes is equivalent to the whole day. Notice the following examples:

- According to Genesis 7:12, the rain of the Noahic Flood was upon the Earth "forty days and forty nights." Verse seventeen of that same chapter says it was on the Earth for just "forty days."

- In Genesis 42:17, Joseph incarcerated his brothers for three days. Then, in verse eighteen, he spoke to them on the third day, and from the context it seems that he released them on that same day—the third day.

- When the people of Israel asked King Rehoboam to lighten their burdens, the king wanted time to contemplate their request, so he instructed Jeroboam and the people of Israel to return "**after** three days" (2 Chronicles 10:5). Verse twelve says that Jeroboam and the people of Israel came to Rehoboam "**on** the third day, as the king had directed, saying, 'Come back to me the third day.' " Fascinating, is it not, that even though Rehoboam instructed his people to return "after three days," they understood this to mean "on the third day."

- In 1 Samuel 30:12-13, the phrases "three days and three nights" and "three days" are used interchangeably.

- When Queen Esther was about to risk her life by going before the king uninvited, she instructed her fellow Jews to follow her example by not eating "for three days, night or day" (Esther 4:16). The text goes on to tell us that Esther went in unto the king "**on** the third day" (5:1, emp. added).

By studying these and other passages, one clearly can see that the Bible uses expressions like "three days," "the third day," "on the third day," "after three days," and "three days and three nights" to signify the same period of time.

Even though in twenty-first-century America some may find this reasoning somewhat confusing, similar idiomatic expressions frequently are used today. For example, we consider a baseball game that ends after only completing 8½ innings a "9-inning game." And even though the losing pitcher on the visiting team only pitched 8 innings (not 9 innings like the winning pitcher from the home team), he is said to have pitched a **complete** game. And what about the man who comes home from work and tells his wife that he was at the office "all day." He may not mean that he worked in the office from sunup to sundown, but rather that the office is where he spent nearly all of his day. And finally, consider the college student who explains to his professor that he worked on a research project "day and night for four weeks." He obviously does not mean that he worked for a solid 672 hours (24 hours x 7 days x 4 weeks) without sleeping. It may be that he worked from 6:00 a.m. to 12:00 a.m. for four weeks on the project, but not 672 sleepless hours. If he slept only five or six hours a night, and worked on the project nearly every hour he was awake, we would consider this person as one who truly did work "day and night for four weeks."

Further evidence proving that Jesus' statements regarding His burial were not contradictory centers on the fact that His enemies never accused Him of contradicting Himself. Certainly this must be because they were quite familiar with the customary flexible method of stating time. In fact, the chief priests and Pharisees even said to Pilate the day after Jesus was crucified: "Sir, we remember, while He was still alive, how that deceiver said, '**After** three days I will rise.' Therefore command that the tomb be made secure **until** the third day" (Matthew 27:63-64, emp. added). The phrase "after three days" must have been equivalent to "the third day," else surely the Pharisees would have asked for a guard of soldiers until the fourth day. Are we surprised that skeptics would charge Jesus with contradicting Himself, yet not level the same charge against the hypocritical Pharisees? Hardly.

The idiomatic expression, "three days and three nights," that Jesus used when comparing His entombment to Jonah's "burial" in a great fish, does not mean that He literally was buried for 72 hours. If we interpret the account of Jesus' crucifixion, burial, and resurrection in light of the cultural setting of the first century, and not according to the present-day (mis)understanding of skeptics, we find no errors in all of the expressions that Jesus and the gospel writers used.

SIX OR EIGHT DAYS?
Matthew 17:1; Mark 9:2; Luke 9:28

After Jesus prophesied during His earthly ministry that some would live to see the establishment of God's kingdom, the first two books of the New Testament indicate **six days** expired before Peter, James, and John were led up on a high mountain to witness the transfiguration of Jesus (Matthew 16:28-17:2; Mark 9:1-2). Luke's account, on the other hand, says that Jesus' transfiguration occurred "about **eight days** after" Jesus prophesied of the approaching kingdom's establishment (9:27-29). Skeptics charge that this difference in the time that elapsed between the two events constitutes an obvious error. They profess that such textual differences should lead the honest person to admit that the Bible contains contradictions, and thus is not the infallible, inerrant Word of God.

Admittedly, at first glance it may seem to the casual reader that Luke's timeline contradicts Matthew and Mark's account of the time that elapsed between Jesus' prophecy and His transfiguration. However, a closer examination reveals that Luke never intended for his readers to understand that exactly 192 hours (eight 24-hour days) elapsed from the moment Jesus finished His prophecy to the time Jesus and the others began their ascent to the "mount of transfiguration." Luke recorded that it was "**about** eight days," not that it was eight days exactly. Although Luke was a physician (cf. Colossians 4:14), he did not use "scientific precision" in this case. He merely approximated the time separating the two events.

Furthermore, it seems clear that whereas Matthew and Mark **excluded** the days of the two terminal events (the prophecy and the transfiguration), Luke **included** both days, as well as the six intermediate days, and thus mentioned that the two events were **eight days** apart. Even today when people rehearse something they witnessed a few days earlier, they may refer to the events as happening on "different" days. For example, if a store was robbed on a Monday afternoon, and the following Monday morning a witness told friends what he had seen, one could say truthfully that he recalled the events six days or eight days after they occurred. If one were counting only full days, then the six would be correct (Tuesday through Sunday). But it also would be correct to speak of the events as occurring eight days earlier–if one were including both full and partial days (Monday through Monday). Whether one uses "six" or "eight" does not discredit his story. Likewise, the time difference between Matthew, Mark, and Luke in no way represents a legitimate contradiction. Luke simply used the inclusive method of reckoning time (counting the portion of a day at either end of the period), whereas Matthew and Mark counted only the complete days (see Coffman, 1971, p. 261).

AT WHAT HOUR WAS JESUS CRUCIFIED?
Mark 15:25; John 19:14

Bible critics have attempted to make much of the fact that whereas the gospel of Mark represents Jesus being crucified at the third hour (Mark 15:25), according to John's account the Lord was still on trial before Pilate at the sixth hour (John 19:14). Supposedly, Mark has Jesus on the cross three hours before John has Him on trial, and thus a genuine contradiction exists because such would be logically impossible.

The truth is, however, this can only be a legitimate contradiction if one assumes that Mark and John were both using the same system of reckoning time. The Jews and the Romans used different standards for calculating the hours of the day, and although both systems split the day into two periods of twelve hours, a new day for the Romans began at midnight (as currently practiced in the West), whereas a new day for the Jews began in the evening at what we would call 6 p.m. The answer to this alleged contradiction is simply that John employed the Roman method of reckoning time (from midnight to midnight), while Mark and the other gospel writers calculated time using the Jewish method (from sundown to sundown).

Various clues within the fourth gospel indicate that John was using Roman time. When he wrote about Jesus arriving at Samaria after His wearisome trip from Judah, John mentioned that Jesus arrived at the "sixth hour," asking for water from the woman at the well (John 4:1-7). Bearing in mind the length of the trip, His exhaustion, and the normal evening time when people went to the well to drink and to water their animals, this fits better with the Roman "sixth hour" (approximately 6:00 p.m.) than with the Jewish "sixth hour" (about noon)

[Geisler and Howe, 1992, p. 376]. A stronger indication that John was using Roman time is seen in his allusion to the **evening** of the resurrection day, **which is still acknowledged as "the first day of the week"** (John 20:19). It seems logical to conclude that if John were using the Jewish method of calculating time, the "evening" of the resurrection day would have been considered the "second" day of the week, not the "first" day.

All of this makes sense, given that: (1) John was probably the last gospel record to be written (near the end of the first century, after Jerusalem was destroyed in A.D. 70); and (2) he likely wrote in or near Ephesus, the capital of the Roman province of Asia Minor, during a time and at a place when the Christian church was predominantly Gentile, not Jewish. That Mark used a Jewish system makes sense in light his agreement with Matthew and Luke on the times of Jesus' trial and crucifixion (cf. Matthew 27:45; Mark 15:33; Luke 23:44). Given this distinction, the "problem" of John's record of the time Jesus was tried before Pilate disappears. John has Pilate handing Jesus over for crucifixion at 6 a.m., and Mark has Jesus on the cross three hours later at 9 a.m. (i.e., "the third hour"). As always, when interpreting the Scriptures, we must take into account the context, as well as cultural differences between the Jewish and Gentile worlds.

HOW LONG WAS THE ISRAELITES' EGYPTIAN SOJOURN?
Acts 7:6; Genesis 15:13; Exodus 6:16-20; 12:40-41

The exact length of the Israelites' "sojourn" has been in the past, and remains today, a matter of much controversy. Certain biblical passages (e.g., Genesis 15:13 and Acts 7:6) seem to indicate a length of **400** years for the time period under consideration. Elsewhere (e.g., Exodus 12:40-41), the length of time appears to be **430** years. Still other information (e.g., 1 Chronicles 6:1, 1 Chronicles 23:6-13, and Exodus 6:16-20) places an upper limit of approximately **350** years on the time frame involved. Can the "apparent disagreements" between these passages be resolved? Yes, they can. However, some background information on each of these passages is required in order to understand the "problems" surrounding them—and the solutions that they provide.

First, the fact must be established that there was a minimum of 215 years between God's promise to Abraham, and the entrance of the Israelites (through Jacob) into Egypt. This figure can be obtained quite readily by reading Genesis 12:4-7; 21:5; 25:26; and 47:9,28. [Abraham was "called" to Canaan at age 75. Two hundred fifteen years later, Jacob entered Egypt.]

Second, the information in passages such as Genesis 46, 1 Chronicles 6:1, 1 Chronicles 23:6-13, and Exodus 6:16-20 places a limitation on the length of the Egyptian sojourn. Again, by way of summary, the information gleaned from these texts is as follows:

- The text in Genesis 46:11 indicates that Kohath, the son of Levi and grandfather of Moses, apparently was born prior to Jacob moving to Egypt with his sons (Genesis 46:11). **If** he had **just been born** at the time, and **if** he sired his son Amram the **last day** of his life, then Amram could have been born no later than 134 years after the entrance into Egypt (rounding a 9-month pregnancy upward to a full year) because Kohath lived only 133 years (Exodus 6:18).

- Amram (the father of Moses) lived 137 years (Exodus 6:20). **If** he had sired Moses the **last day** of his life, then Moses would have been born no more than 272 years after Jacob and his sons entered Egypt (133 +1 + 137 + 1 = 272).

- Moses was 80 years old when Israel came out of Egypt (Exodus 7:7).

- Add that 80 to the 272, and the total is a maximum of 352 years.

- Additional information that delimits the number of years of the sojourn can be derived from a source completely independent of Kohath—Moses' mother, Jochebed. The Bible mentions her twice, the first instance being Exodus 6:20: "And Amram took him Jochebed his father's sister to wife; and she bare him Aaron and Moses: and the years of the life of Amram were a hundred and thirty and seven years." Jochebed is named a second time in Numbers 26:59: "And the name of Amram's wife was Jochebed, the daughter of Levi, who was born to Levi in Egypt: and she bare unto Amram Aaron and Moses, and Miriam their sister."

Clearly, Jochebed (who was born in Egypt) was the daughter of Levi, the sister of Kohath. With this information before us, let's "crunch the numbers." Eleven of Jacob's sons were born within a seven-year period. Remember that as a bachelor, Jacob worked seven years for Laban in order to "pay" for Rachel, but was tricked by Laban into marrying Leah (Genesis 29). Then, he worked for seven more years in order to marry Rachel. At the end of this second seven years, he asked to depart from Laban with all of the children who had been born to him and his wives (Genesis 30:25). With Levi being the third son of Jacob/Leah (allowing approximately one year for the births of Reuben, Simeon, and Levi), he could have been only about four years older than Joseph, who was born near the end of the seven-year period. As Joseph was 39 when Jacob came into Egypt (he was 30 when he appeared before Pharaoh [Genesis 41:46], plus seven years of plenty, plus one more year before the famine was realized), Levi could not have been more than 44 or 45 when he came into Egypt. Levi lived in Egypt for 93 years (his age at his death was 137 [Exodus 6:16], minus 44 [his age when he went into Egypt], which equals 93).

If Levi had conceived Jochebed **on the very last day of his life**, then **Jochebed would have had to have given birth to Moses when she was 257 years old** in order to get a period of 430 years for the sojourn in Egypt (93 years that Levi lived in Egypt, plus Moses' 80 years (Exodus 7:7) when he arrived to deliver the children of Israel–93+80+257=430). Recalling the fact that Sarah was "only" 90 when the miraculous birth of Isaac occurred, it makes little sense to suggest that Jochebed gave birth to Moses when she was almost three times as old as Sarah! Furthermore, we know that life spans were far shorter than 257 by this time, and that the 430-year sojourn does not (and cannot) fit with the genealogies–either through Kohath or through Jochebed.

Where, then, do the figures of 430 years and 400 years fit into all of this? Were the Israelites in Egypt 645 years? Or 430 years? Or 400 years? Or 215 years?

As I attempt to provide the answers to such questions, it must be pointed out that **no one** has stepped forward to suggest that the Israelites were in Egypt for **645 years.** Such a view is indefensible in light of the biblical evidence, including (but not necessarily limited to) the scripturally imposed time limit mentioned above of 352 years. There are, however, two major viewpoints regarding the specific length of Israel's sojourn. The first suggests that the Israelites **actually lived in Egypt** for 430 years (cf. Exodus 12:40-41). The second claims that the Israelites were in Egypt for only 215 years, not 430.

Those who suggest that the sojourn lasted only 215 years believe that the time period of "the sojourning of the children of Israel" **begins with the call of Abraham** and God's promise to him (Genesis 12:1-3), **and ends with the Exodus.** In other words, the fathers (Abraham, Isaac, and Jacob) sojourned in Canaan for 215 years, and their descendants lived in Egyptian bondage for an additional 215 years. The total, then, is the 430-year figure of Exodus 12:40-41 (and Galatians 3:17). But how can the 215-year figure be defended?

First, it must be admitted forthrightly, in light of the information given above, that there is a **maximum** of 352 years available for the sojourn in Egypt, whatever that sojourn might encompass. There simply is no way around that fact.

Second, Paul, in his epistle to the Galatians, reviewed the time element associated with the covenant between God and Abraham (given in Genesis 15) when he wrote:

> Now to Abraham were the promises spoken, and to his seed. He saith not, "And to seeds," as of many; but as of one, "And to thy seed," which is Christ. Now this I say: A covenant confirmed beforehand by God, the law—which came **four hundred and thirty years after**—doth not disannul, so as to make the promise of none effect (3:16-17).

If the time period between Abraham's call and the giving of the law (which occurred roughly three months after the Exodus) was 430 years (and Paul specifically remarked that it was), and if 215 of those years had passed **before** the Israelites went into Egypt (the time period from Abraham's call to Jacob's entrance into the land of the Nile), then that would leave only 215 years remaining for the Israelites' sojourn in Egypt—which is exactly the time frame I believe the evidence supports.

Third, in Genesis 15:16 it was prophesied that the Israelites would return to Palestine during the lifetime of the "fourth generation"—which they did, according to Exodus 6:16-20, Numbers 3:17-19, Numbers 26:57-59, 1 Chronicles 6:1-3, and 1 Chronicles 23:6,12-13 (Jacob-Levi-Kohath-Amram-Moses). As Harold Hoehner admitted: "To fit four generations into a 215-year period is much more reasonable than a 430-year span" (1969, 126:309).

Fourth, there are important historical and/or textual considerations that need to be investigated in this matter. For example, in *Antiquities of the Jews,* Josephus wrote that the Israelites "left Egypt in the month of Xanthicus, on the fifteenth day of the lunar month; four hundred and thirty years after our forefather Abraham came into Canaan, but **two hundred and fifteen years only after Jacob removed into Egypt**" (Book 2, Chapter 15, Section 2). In the Masoretic text of the Old Testament, Exodus 12:40 reads as follows: "The time that the children of Israel dwelt in Egypt was **four hundred and thirty years**." Two other highly reliable biblical texts, however, strongly suggest that this translation is incorrect due to a critical omission. In both the Samaritan Pentateuch and the Septuagint (the Greek translation of the Old Testament), Exodus 12:40 reads as follows: "Now the sojourning of the children of Israel **and of their fathers**, which they sojourned **in the land of Canaan AND in the land of Egypt** was 430 years" (see Clarke, n.d., pp. 358-359, emp. in orig.). Egyptologist David Rohl has suggested that it really is not hard to understand why the Masorete copy abridges the account in Exodus 12:40 so as to ascribe 430 years solely to the Israelites' sojourn in Egypt, rather than their pilgrimage in Canaan and Egypt. In fact, he said:

> It is fairly easy to see what happened in the interval between Josephus' day and that of the Masoretes. During the process of copying down the original scrolls over the intervening centuries, a section of text something on the lines of "and in the land of Canaan" had fallen out (or had been edited out). This is confirmed by the Greek rendition of the Old Testament (the Septuagint or LXX) which retains the original, full version of the passage (1995, p. 331).

In his commentary on the Pentateuch, Adam Clarke discussed this at length:

...the Samaritan Pentateuch, by preserving the two passages, **they and their fathers** and **in the land of Canaan**, which are lost out of the present copies of the Hebrew text, has rescued this passage from all obscurity and contradiction. It may be necessary to observe that the Alexandrian copy of the Septuagint has the same reading as that in the Samaritan. The Samaritan Pentateuch is allowed by many learned men to exhibit the most correct copy of the five books of Moses; and the Alexandrian copy of the Septuagint must also be allowed to be one of the most authentic as well as most ancient copies of this version which we possess (n.d., pp. 358-359, emp. in orig.).

If Josephus, the Samaritan Pentateuch, and the Septuagint are correct (and there is good evidence to indicate that they are) in stating that "the sojourning of the children of Israel **and of their fathers**, which they sojourned **in the land of Canaan AND in the land of Egypt** was 430 years," then the alleged contradiction between Exodus 12:40-41 and Galatians 3:17 evaporates into thin air, and the 215-year figure for the Israelites' sojourn in Egypt can be accepted quite easily as both credible and scriptural.

But where do the "400 years" of Genesis 15:13 and Acts 7:6 fit into this scheme? As God spoke to Abraham in Genesis 15 (while the patriarch was dwelling among the terebinth trees at Hebron), the Lord said: "Know of a surety that thy seed shall be sojourners in a land that is not theirs, and shall serve them; and they shall afflict them **four hundred years**" (ASV). Here, God was permitting His faithful servant—through words spoken approximately two centuries **prior** to Israel's entrance into Egypt—to peek into the future of his descendants. Add to that the words of Stephen (in Acts 7:6) when he said, looking back on Israel's history: "And God spake on this wise, that his seed should sojourn in a strange land, and that they should bring them into bondage, and treat them ill, **four hundred years**" (ASV). What is the meaning of these particular passages?

Some writers have suggested that the 400-year figure represents merely a "rounding off" of the 430-year figure given in Genesis 15:13. But a better explanation suggests that there is a **fundamental distinction** between the 430-year figure and the 400-year figure.

Notice that in Stephen's speech he specifically stated that Abraham's "**seed** should sojourn in a strange land." In his book, *The Wonders of Bible Chronology,* Philip Mauro wrote:

> The period of 430 years includes the sojourn of Abram and Sarah. That of 400, however, begins with the experience of Abraham's "seed." This refers, of course, to Isaac in the first place; for in Isaac the promised "seed" was to be "called"; but the era is not that of the **birth** of Isaac, but that when he was acknowledged the "seed" and the "heir" by the casting out of Hagar and Ishmael. That took place at the time of the "great feast" which Abraham made the day Isaac was weaned (Gen. 21: 8-10). This is an important event in the annals of God's people, because of its deep spiritual significance, as appears by the reference to it in Galatians 4:29,30.

> From the foregoing Scriptures we are able to arrive at the date when Isaac was weaned and Ishmael was cast out (whereby Isaac became the acknowledged "seed" and "heir"). For there is a difference of thirty years between the two periods. But we have already found that there were twenty-five years from the call of Abraham (and God's "covenant" with him) to the birth of Isaac. Hence, deducting 25 from 30 gives us 5 years as the age of Isaac when Ishmael was cast out. There is no need to give at greater length the proofs concerning the 400-year period (n.d., pp. 27-28, emp. in orig.).

Professor Hoehner agreed with Mauro, saying, "The 400 years was from the weaning of Isaac to the time of the Exodus" (1969, 126:309).

Some may ask, though, how the 215-year figure for the Israelites' time in Egypt can be squared with statements such as those in Genesis 15:13 and Acts 7:6, which seem to indicate that the Hebrews would be "sojourners **in a strange land that is not theirs**" where their enemies would "**bring them into bondage**" and "**treat them ill**"? In his commentary on Galatians, David Lipscomb addressed this point.

> The law was given by Moses four hundred and thirty years after this promise was made to Abraham (Ex. 12:40). Many interpret this to mean that they sojourned in Egypt four hundred and thirty years. **But they dwelt in tents and had no permanent habitation** during their sojourn in Canaan and Egypt and in the wilderness from the call in Ur until the entrance into Canaan after the Egyptian bondage (n.d., p. 231, emp. added).

Abraham, Sarah, and their children were strangers and pilgrims while living in Canaan (Hebrews 11:8-13). In Exodus 6:4, **Canaan** is referred to as "the land in which they dwelt **as sojourners**." While it certainly is true that they were slaves in Egypt for a considerable period of time (215 years), their oppression actually began much earlier, and lasted much longer, than just those 215 years. In fact, it would be accurate to say that the oppression began as early as Ishmael, who was half Egyptian and who mocked Isaac, the son of promise (Genesis 21:9). In Galatians 4:29, Paul discussed Ishmael's ill treatment of Isaac when he penned these words: "He that was born after the flesh persecuted him that was born after the Spirit." That "persecution" obviously continued, as is evident from the fact that Egyptians felt it was a great abomination to eat with Hebrews (Genesis 43:32)—even until the time that Joseph came to power in their country. Later, of course, the persecution culminated in the attempted destruction by Pharaoh of the Hebrew male babies during Moses' infancy (Exodus

1:15-22). Thus, the "sojourning" and "ill treatment" did not occur **only** during Egyptian captivity, but actually had commenced much earlier.

Critics of the 215-year view, however, have suggested that the second 215-year period (i.e., the time spent in Egypt) would not allow for the population explosion that obviously occurred while the Hebrews were captives. Less than 100 went down into Egypt, and yet by the time they left, they numbered roughly 2 million or more (based on the figures in Numbers 1:46). However, C.G. Ozanne, in his volume, *The First 7,000 Years,* has shed some light on this criticism.

> Of course, the standard objection to this interpretation is the census totals of male Levites in Numbers 3. In this chapter the total number of Kohath's male descendants "from a month old and upward" is given as 8600 (v. 28), these being divided between his four sons, Amram, Izhar, Hebron, and Uzziel. Assuming that the total number is to be divided evenly between the four sons, Amram must have had some 2150 male descendants within a few months of the Exodus. At first sight this figure may seem well-nigh impossible. When, however, it is broken down, it begins to assume more reasonable proportions. Thus, supposing that Amram was born fifty-five years after the descent into Egypt and that forty years constitute a generation, it is only necessary to allocate seven males to a family to arrive at a figure considerably in excess of the desired 2150. On this reckoning Moses would have had 7 brothers (for he himself may be ignored for the purposes of this calculation), 49 nephews, 343 great-nephews and 2401 great-great-nephews within the allotted span. A total of 2800 is thus obtained, of which the vast majority would still have been alive to see the exodus from Egypt. Bearing in mind the greatly extended period of childbearing (Jochebed was about

70 at the birth of Moses), the practice of polygamy (which enabled Jacob to have eleven sons in seven years), and above all the astonishing fertility of the Israelite women on which the Bible lays special emphasis (cf. Gen. 46.3; Exod. 1.7,12,19; Deut. 26.5), the rate of increase here suggested should not necessarily be thought incredible (1970, pp. 22-23).

When **all** of the biblical information is considered, it is apparent that there is no contradiction between Exodus 12:40-41 and Galatians 3:17. Nor is there any problem in regard to Genesis 15:13 and Acts 7:6.

Chapter 7

THE REALITY OF COPYISTS' ERRORS

From time to time, a person reading the Bible will come across names or numbers in two or more passages that seem to contradict each other. After thoroughly studying the context of the passages in order to make certain that the assumed contradiction is not just a misunderstanding of the text, the reader then concludes that the passages do indeed contradict one another. For example, 2 Kings 24:8 says that Jehoiachin succeeded his father as the nineteenth king of Judah at the age of **eighteen**, whereas 2 Chronicles 36:9 informs us that he was "**eight** years old when he became king." The honest person must admit that these two passages are in disagreement. The question that must be asked is: Do such disagreements indicate that the Bible is not the inspired Word of God? No, they do not.

The fact is, differences within two or more biblical accounts **may** be the result of copyists' errors. Oftentimes, modern man forgets that whenever duplicates of the Old Testament Scriptures were needed, copies had to be made by hand—a painstaking, time-consuming task requiring extreme concentration and special working conditions. In time, an elite group of scribes,

known as the Masoretes, arose just for this purpose. Norman
Geisler and William Nix, in their classic work on critical biblical issues, *A General Introduction to the Bible*, observed:

> The Masoretic period (flourished c. A.D. 500-1000)
> of Old Testament manuscript copying indicates a com-
> plete review of established rules, a deep reverence
> for the Scriptures, and a systematic renovation of trans-
> mission techniques…. Copies were made by an offi-
> cial class of sacred scribes who labored under strict
> rules (1986, pp. 354,467; cf. also pp. 371,374,380).

The Masoretes went "above and beyond the call of duty" in
order to make the most accurate copies humanly possible.
Out of respect for the Word of God, these copyists took numerous precautions to "guarantee" precise duplication. As
Eddie Hendrix noted:

> When a scribe finally completed the laborious task
> of copying it with a catalog of detailed information
> about that book, the catalog listed the number of
> verses, words, and letters that should occur in the book.
> The catalog also listed the word and the letter that
> should fall in the middle of the book. Such minute
> checks contributed to a high degree of copying ac-
> curacy (1976, p. 5).

Anyone who has studied the exacting conditions under which
the Masoretes worked, and the lengths to which they went
to ensure fidelity in their copies of the Scriptures, could at-
test to the fact that their goal was to produce accurate copies—even to the point of reproducing errors already present
in the much older copies from which they were working. The
Masoretes were some of the world's greatest perfectionists.
They were, nevertheless, still human.

There are at least seven important ways in which a copyist
might change the text accidentally, including such actions as:
(a) omissions of letters, words, or whole lines; (b) unwarranted

repetitions; (c) transposition (the reversal of two letters or words); (d) errors of memory; (e) errors of the ear; (f) errors of the eye; and (g) errors of judgment (Geisler and Nix, 1986, pp. 469-473).

Such errors, especially before the Masoretes came on the scene, could account for the alleged discrepancies in various parts of the Bible (cf. 1 Kings 4:26; 2 Kings 8:26; 2 Chronicles 9:25; 22:2). For example, biblical scholar Gleason Archer has stated: "Even the earliest and best manuscripts that we possess are not totally free of transmissional errors. Numbers are occasionally miscopied, the spelling of proper names is occasionally garbled, and there are examples of the same types of scribal error that appear in other ancient documents as well" (1982, p. 27). Do copyists' errors appear in other ancient documents, too? Most assuredly! Corruptions in the writings of the Greek classics are very common. Take, for instance, the secular works of Tacitus. They are known to contain at least one numerical error that Tacitean and classical scholars have acknowledged as a copyist's mistake (Holding, 2001). These scholars recognize that, at some point in history, a copyist accidentally changed a number (from CXXV to XXV). Why is it, then, that biblical critics will not recognize the same possibility when supposed discrepancies are found in the Bible? Just as those who copied secular historical documents sometimes misspelled names and numbers, scribes who copied the Bible from earlier texts occasionally made mistakes. The complexity of the Hebrew language and its alphabetic/numeric system no doubt served as an even greater challenge for the scribes.

Errors of the ear also may have played a part. If a scribe was writing the text as it was being read to him, the reader actually may have **said** one thing while the scribe **heard** another. Other differences might have been the result of an error of memory. A scribe may have looked at an entire line, memorized it, and copied it from memory without looking at it a second time during the copying process. When he went to write one of the numbers in the two passages, however, his memory failed him; what he **thought** he remembered the original text having said was not what it **actually** said. Such could have been the case in 2 Chronicles 22:2, where it says that Ahaziah was forty-two years old when he became king of Judah. In light of other Scriptures (2 Kings 8:17,26), one understands that Ahaziah could not have been forty-two when he inherited the throne, because this would make him two years older than his father. The correct reading of Ahaziah's age is "twenty-two" (2 Kings 8:17), not "forty-two." When one stops to consider the extremely poor conditions under which most copyists worked (poor lighting, crude writing instruments, imperfect writing surfaces, etc.), it is not difficult to understand how inadvertent errors such as these might occur from time to time.

Is God to be blamed for these errors? Although some would like to think so, one must remember that an author is not responsible for errors that are found in copies made of his book. God cannot be blamed for errors made by those who have copied the Scriptures in the distant past. Nor can He be held accountable for those who continue to print copies of the Bible today. It is not God's fault that various publishing companies today have printed translations of the Bible containing such things as misspelled words, incorrect numbers, duplicate words, etc. Would it be God's fault if I decided to copy the whole Bible by hand, with the result being a copy of the Bible containing some misspelled names and a few wrong numbers? Certainly not! God is not responsible for the errors made by those who produce copies of the Bible.

But why is it, then, that we do not possess infallible copies of the infallible originals of the Bible books? Archer has observed that it is

> because the production of even one perfect copy of one book is so far beyond the capacity of a human scribe as to render it necessary for God to perform a miracle in order to produce it. No reasonable person can expect even the most conscientious copyist to achieve technical infallibility in transcribing his original document into a fresh copy.... But the important fact remains that accurate communication is possible despite technical mistakes in copying (1982, p. 29).

Indeed, **accurate** communication **is** possible despite technical mistakes in copying. In the more than two decades during which Apologetics Press has published its monthly journal, *Reason and Revelation*, we never have had someone suggest that as a result of an inadvertent mistake they were unable to comprehend the meaning, or detect the intent, of an article. Cannot the same be said of the Bible? Surely it can! Archer concluded:

> Well-trained textual critics operating on the basis of sound methodology are able to rectify almost all misunderstandings that might result from manuscript error.... Is there objective proof from the surviving manuscripts of Scripture that these sixty-six books have been transmitted to us with such a high degree of accuracy as to assure us that the information contained in the originals has been perfectly preserved? The answer is an unqualified yes (pp. 29-30).

In every case when the Bible's defenders refer to that Grand Book as being "inspired," they are by necessity referring to inspiration as it pertained to the original manuscripts (routinely referred to as "autographs"), since there is no such thing as an "inspired copy." "Aha!," the skeptic might say, "since you no longer possess those autographs, but only slightly flawed copies made by imperfect humans, that makes it impossible to know the truth of the message behind the text."

Try applying such a concept—that no longer being in personal possession of a perfect original makes knowing truth impossible—to matters of everyday life. Gleason Archer has done just that, using something as simple as a yardstick.

> It is wrong to affirm that the existence of a perfect original is a matter of no importance if that original is no longer available for examination. To take an example from the realm of engineering or of commerce, it makes a very great difference whether there is such a thing as a perfect measure for the meter, the foot, or the pound. It is questionable whether the yardsticks or scales used in business transactions or construction projects can be described as absolutely perfect. They may be almost completely conformable to the standard weights and measures preserved at the Bureau of Standards in our nation's capital but they are subject to error—however small. But how foolish it would be for any citizen to shrug his shoulders and say, "Neither you nor I have ever actually seen those standard measures in Washington; therefore we may as well disregard them—not be concerned about them at all—and simply settle realistically for the imperfect yardsticks and pound weights that we have available to us in everyday life." On the contrary, the existence of those measures in the Bureau of Standards is vital to the proper functioning of our entire economy. To the 222,000,000 Americans who have never seen them they are absolutely essential for the trustworthiness of all the standards of measurement that they resort to throughout their lifetime (p. 28).

The fact that we do not possess the original autographs of the Bible in no way diminishes the usefulness, or authority, of the copies, any more than a construction superintendent not being in possession of the original measures from the Bureau of Standards diminishes the usefulness or authority of the devices he employs to erect a building. This point is made all the more evident when one considers the inconsequential nature of the vast majority of alleged discrepancies offered by skeptics as proof of the Bible's non-divine origin. Does not the "quality" of the "discrepancies" submitted to us by skeptics reveal just how desperate skepticism is to try to find **some** discrepancy—**any** discrepancy—within the Sacred Text? But to what end? As Archer noted:

> In fact, it has long been recognized by the foremost specialists in textual criticism that if any decently attested variant were taken up from the apparatus at the bottom of the page and were substituted for the accepted reading of the standard text, there would in no case be a single, significant alteration in doctrine or message (p. 30).

Most Bible critics are completely indifferent to the principles of textual criticism. They disregard rules of interpretation, and treat the Bible differently than any other historical document. These skeptics assume that partial reports of an event are false reports, that figurative language must be interpreted literally, and that numbers always must be exact and never estimated. But the most frustrating truth for skeptics to accept involves copyists' errors. Even though textual critics in secular studies readily acknowledge such errors when studying the writings of historians like Josephus, Tacitus, or Seutonius, critics of the Bible hypocritically reject the explanations involving copyists' errors.

EXAMPLES OF COPYISTS' ERRORS
Who Killed Goliath? (2 Samuel 21:19; 1 Chronicles 20:5)

Some might be surprised to learn that an alleged contradiction hovers over one of the most famous battles ever to have taken place on the Earth—the clash between David and Goliath. Whereas, in 1 Samuel 17 the detailed record clearly shows that David defeated the defiant Philistine giant (Goliath), 2 Samuel 21:19 says that Goliath was kill by "**Elhanan**, the son of Jaare-oregim the Beth-lehemite" (ASV). Furthermore, 1 Chronicles 20:5 states that "Elhanan the son of Jair killed Lahmi **the brother of Goliath** the Gittite, the shaft of whose spear was like a weaver's beam." So who actually killed Goliath? And how does Elhanan fit into all of this?

First, we must recognize that Jair and Jaareoregim are the same person. The widely quoted Albert Barnes noted that this difficulty may have begun when *oregim*, the Hebrew word translated "weaver" in this passage, ended up being placed on the wrong line by a copyist—something that has been known to happen in several instances (see Spence and Exell, 1978, 4: 514). Therefore, Jair, combined with *oregim*, became *Jaare-oregim* in order to make it fit with proper Hebrew grammar.

Second, the phrase "Lahmi the brother of" is absent in 2 Samuel 21:19. [The King James Version inserts the phrase "the brother of" between "Bethlehemite" and "Goliath."] In the Hebrew, *eth Lachmi* (a combination of "Lahmi" and the term "brother") appears to have been changed into *beith hallachmi* (Beth-lehemite) in 2 Samuel 21:19. With this simple correction, the two texts would be in clear agreement (Clarke, 1996). In other words, **"the brother of" and the name "Lahmi" likely were mistakenly combined by a copyist to form what is translated in English as "Beth-lehemite" in 2 Samuel 21:19**. Thus, "the 2 Samuel 21 passage is a perfectly traceable corruption of the original wording, which fortunately has been correctly preserved in 1 Chronicles 20:5" (Archer, p. 179). David slew Goliath, while Elhanan killed Goliath's brother. A fair, in-depth examination of the alleged difficulty shows that there actually is no contradiction at all, but simply a copyist's mistake.

How Old was Jehoiachin when He Began His Reign? (2 Kings 24:8; 2 Chronicles 36:9)

In Second Kings 24:8, we read that Jehoiachin succeeded his father as the nineteenth king of Judah at the age of **eighteen.** Second Chronicles 36:9 informs us that he was "**eight** years old when he became king." Fortunately there is enough additional information in the biblical text to prove the correct age of Jehoiachin when he began his reign over Judah.

There is little doubt that Jehoiachin began his reign at eighteen, not eight years of age. This conclusion is established by Ezekiel 19:5-9, where Jehoiachin appears as going up and down among the lions, catching the prey, devouring men, and knowing the widows of the men he devoured and the cities he wasted. As Keil and Delitzsch observed when commenting on this passage: "The knowing of widows cannot apply to a boy of eight, but might well be said of a young man of eighteen." Furthermore, it is doubtful that an eight-year child would be described as one having done "evil in the sight of the Lord" (2 Kings 24:9).

The simple answer to this "problem" is that a copyist, **not an inspired writer**, made a mistake. A scribe simply omitted a ten, which made Jehoiachin eight instead of eighteen. This does not mean the Bible had errors in the original autographs, but it does indicate that minor scribal errors have slipped into some copies of the Bible. [If you have ever seen the Hebrew alphabet, you no doubt recognize that the Hebrew letters (which were used for numbers) could be confused quite easily.]

Hadadezer or Hadarezer? (2 Samuel 8:3,16,19; 1 Chronicles 18:3; KJV and ASV)

This discrepancy obviously came about through the mistake of a scribe. It is very likely that Hadadezer (with a "d") is the true form since, "Hadad was the chief idol, or sun-god, of the Syrians" (Barnes, 1997; cf. Benhadad and Hadad of 1 Kings 15:18; 11:14; etc.). As William Arndt stated: "D and R may be distinct enough in appearance in English, but in Hebrew they are vexingly similar to each other" (1955, p. XV). There should be no doubt in our minds that Hadarezer simply is a corrupted form of Hadadezer. Surely, one can see how a copyist could easily have made this mistake.

When did Absalom Commit Treason? (2 Samuel 15:7)

When David's son Absalom finally returned after killing his half-brother Amnon, 2 Samuel 15 indicates that "after forty years" passed, Absalom left home again and committed treason. Anyone who knows much Israelite history quickly realizes that Absalom most certainly did not spend 40 years at home during this time, for David's entire reign was only 40 years (2 Samuel 5:4). The number given in 2 Samuel 15:7 probably should be **four years**, which is more in keeping with the lifetime of Absalom, who was born in Hebron after David's reign as king began (2 Samuel 3:3). The number "four" also agrees with such ancient versions as the Septuagint, the Syriac, the Arabic, and the Vulgate. There is little question that the number "forty" represents a copyist error.

How Many Stalls did Solomon have? (1 Kings 4:26; 2 Chronicles 9:25)

First Kings 4:26 indicates that Solomon owned 40,000 stalls. However in 2 Chronicles 9:25 the number 4,000 is given. Both numbers obviously cannot be correct. Likely, respected biblical commentators Keil and Delitzsch were correct when they stated that the forty thousand figure in 1 Kings 4:26 "is an old copyist's error" (1996, p. 39). We learn elsewhere in the books of 1 Kings and 2 Chronicles that Solomon's chariots were but 1,400 (10:26; 1:14). It makes sense then that 40,000 horses could not possibly be required. In a way of comparison, Albert Barnes indicated that the "Assyrian chariots had at most three horses apiece, while some had only two. 4,000 horses would supply the full team of three to 1,200 and the smaller team of two to

2000 chariots" (1997). The 4,000 figure appears to be the more probable of the two renderings.

IS THE OLD TESTAMENT
STILL RELIABLE?

If there are scribal errors in today's copies of the Old Testament, many wonder how we can be certain the text of the Bible was transmitted faithfully across the centuries? Is it not possible that it was corrupted so that its form in our present Bible is drastically different from the original source?

The accuracy of the Old Testament text was demonstrated forcefully by the discovery of the Dead Sea scrolls. Prior to 1947, the oldest Hebrew manuscripts of significant length did not date earlier than the ninth century A.D. However, when the Dead Sea scrolls were found (containing portions of all Old Testament books except Esther), this discovery pushed the record of the Old Testament text back almost 1,000 years. These copies were produced sometime between 200 B.C. and A.D. 100. One scroll found in the Qumran caves was of particular importance. It was a scroll of the book of Isaiah, which only had a few words missing. What was amazing about this scroll is that when it was compared to the text of Isaiah produced 900 years after it, the two matched almost word for word with only a few small variations. In commenting on this comparative reading of the two texts, A.W. Adams observed:

> The close agreement of the second Isaiah Scroll from the Dead Sea with the manuscripts of the ninth and tenth centuries shows how carefully the text tradition which they represent has been preserved.

> We may therefore be satisfied that the text of our Old Testament has been handed down in one line without serious change since the beginning of the Christian era and even before (as quoted by Kenyon, 1939, pp. 69,88).

Amazingly, a comparison of the standard Hebrew texts with that of the Dead Sea scrolls has revealed that the two are virtually identical. The variations (about 5%) occurred only in minor spelling differences and minute copyists' mistakes. Thus, as Rene Paché noted: "Since it can be demonstrated that the text of the old Testament was accurately transmitted for the last 2,000 years, one may reasonably suppose that it had been so transmitted from the beginning" (1971, p. 191).

Even within the various passages of Scripture, numerous references to copies of the written Word of God can be found. [It would be a gratuitous conclusion to assume that only one copy of the Scriptures existed during the period that the Old Testament covers.] A copy of the "book of the law" was preserved in the temple during the days of king Josiah (c. 621 B.C.), thus demonstrating that Moses' writings had been protected over a span of almost 1,000 years (2 Kings 22). Other Old Testament passages speak of the maintenance of the Holy Writings across the years (Jeremiah 36; Ezra 7:14; Nehemiah 8: 1-18).

During Jesus' personal ministry, He read from the Isaiah scroll in the synagogue at Nazareth and called it "Scripture" (Luke 4:16-21)—a technical term always employed in the Bible for a **divine** writing! Jesus endorsed the truth that the Old Testament Scriptures had been preserved faithfully. Even though Jesus read from a **copy** of Isaiah, He still considered it the Word of God. Hence, Scripture had been preserved faithfully in **written** form. Furthermore, even though Jesus condemned the scribes of His day for their many sins, not one instance in Scripture is it recorded where He even intimated they were unfaithful in their work as scribes. Yes, Jesus gave approval to copies (and translations—e.g., Septuagint) of the Old Testament by reading and quoting from them. We should do no less.

One of the great language scholars of the Old Testament text was Dr. Robert Dick Wilson (1856-1930). A master of over thirty-five languages, Wilson carefully compared the text of the Old Testament with inscriptions on ancient monuments (as these two sources dealt with common material). As a result of his research, he declared that "we are scientifically certain that we have substantially the same text that was in the possession of Christ and the apostles and, so far as anybody knows, the same as that written by the original composers of the Old Testament documents" (1929, p. 8).

For the believer, it is only logical to conclude that if a just God exists (Psalm 89:14; cf. 19:1), and if He expects man to obey Him (Hebrews 5:8-9; John 14:15), then His Will must be preserved. Since man is amenable to God's religious and moral laws, it surely follows that God, through His providence, would preserve accurate copies of His divine Will in order that those who are created "in the image of God" (Genesis 1:27) might be able to avoid the consequences of disobedience and have access to the wonderful blessings in Jesus Christ (cf. 2 Timothy 2:10). How could we do this if we did not have access to accurate copies of the Bible?

WHAT ABOUT THE RELIABILITY OF THE NEW TESTAMENT?

How well do the New Testament documents compare with additional ancient, historical documents? F.F Bruce examined much of the evidence surrounding this question in his book, *The New Testament Documents—Are They Reliable?* As he and other writers (e.g., Metzger, 1968, p. 36; Geisler and Brooks, 1990, p. 159) have noted, there are over 5,300 manuscripts of the Greek New Testament in existence today, in whole or in part, that serve to corroborate the accuracy of the New Testament. The best manuscripts of the New Testament are dated at roughly A.D. 350, with perhaps one of the most important of these being the Codex Vaticanus, "the chief treasure of the Vatican

Library in Rome," and the Codex Sinaiticus, which was purchased by the British from the Soviet Government in 1933 (Bruce, 1953, p. 20). Additionally, the Chester Beatty papyri, made public in 1931, contain eleven codices (manuscript volumes), three of which contain most of the New Testament (including the gospel accounts). Two of these codices boast a date in the first half of the third century, while the third slides in a little later, being dated in the last half of the same century (Bruce, p. 21). The John Rylands Library boasts even earlier evidence. A papyrus codex containing parts of John 18 dates to the time of Hadrian, who reigned from A.D. 117 to 138 (Bruce, p. 21).

Other attestation to the accuracy of the New Testament documents can be found in the writings of the so-called "apostolic fathers"–men who wrote primarily from A.D. 90 to 160, and who often quoted from the New Testament documents (Bruce, p. 22). Irenaeus, Clement of Alexandria, Tertullian, Tatian, Clement of Rome, and Ignatius (writing before the close of the second century) all provided citations from one or more of the gospel accounts (Guthrie, 1990, p. 24). Other witnesses to the authenticity of the New Testament are the Ancient Versions, which consist of the text of the New Testament translated into different languages. The Old Latin and the Old Syriac are the most ancient, being dated from the middle of the second century (Bruce, p. 23).

The fact is, the New Testament enjoys far more historical documentation than any other volume ever known. Compared to the 5,300+ Greek manuscripts "backing" the New Testament, there are only 643 copies of Homer's *Iliad*, which is undeniably the most famous book of ancient Greece. No one doubts the text of Julius Caesar's *Gallic Wars*, but we have only 10 copies of it, the earliest of which was made 1,000 years after it was written. We have only two manuscripts of Tacitus' *Histories* and *Annals*, one from the ninth century and one from the eleventh. The *History of Thucydides*, another well-known ancient work, is dependent upon only eight manuscripts, the oldest of these being dated about A.D. 900 (along with a few papyrus scraps dated at the beginning of the Christian era). And *The History of Herodotus* finds itself in a similar situation. "Yet no classical scholar would listen to an argument that the authenticity of Herodotus or Thucydides is in doubt because the earliest MSS [manuscripts–EL] of their works which are of any use to us are over 1,300 years later than the originals" (Bruce, pp. 20-21). Bruce thus declared: "It is a curious fact that historians have often been much readier to trust the New Testament records than have many theologians" (p. 19). In 1968, Bruce Metzger, a longtime professor of New Testament language and literature at Princeton, stated: "The amount of evidence for the text of the New Testament…is so much greater than that available for any ancient classical author that the necessity of resorting to emendation is reduced to the smallest dimensions" (1968, p. 86). Truly, to have such abundance of copies for the New Testament from within seventy years of their writing is nothing short of amazing (see Geisler and Brooks, 1990, pp. 159-160).

The available evidence makes it clear that the New Testament has been transmitted accurately over the past 2,000 years, with relatively few variations. Consider this: Since the King James Version was first translated (in 1611) and revised (one of the latest revisions taking place in 1769), several manuscripts came to light that were older than those used in the KJV translation. When these manuscripts were compared and contrasted with those used in the translation of the KJV, the Greek text used in its translation was seen to be essentially sound. Although the translators of the American Standard Version (published in 1901) had access to more ancient Greek manuscripts than did the KJV translators, the ASV differs very little from the KJV. And since most differences are seen only in the matter of vocabulary choices, someone reading from the KJV has no difficulty listening to a person reading from the ASV. The truth is, if the English language were not constantly changing, there likely would be no need for more translations of the Bible. We can be confident that we have accurate copies of the New Testament today—a fact attested to by more than 5,000 manuscripts of the Greek New Testament.

Chapter 8

ALLEGED GENEALOGICAL CONTRADICTIONS

HOW OLD WAS TERAH WHEN ABRAHAM WAS BORN?

Genesis 11:26, 32; 12:4; Acts 7:4

Unfortunately, in an attempt to defend the strict chronology of Bible genealogies, there are some who read them without taking into account that certain Hebrew phrases possess a wider connotation than what might be perceived in English. One of these phrases is found several times in Genesis 11. In this chapter, we learn of various Messianic ancestors who **lived a certain age** and **begot sons**. For example, verse 16 of that chapter reads: "Eber lived thirty-four years, and begot Peleg." Later, we read where "Nahor lived 29 years, and begot Terah" (11:24). The sons listed in this chapter are generally thought to be the firstborn sons, yet the evidence shows that this was not always the case because there was **not** always a father-to-**firstborn**-son linkage.

Many have assumed that because Genesis 11:26 states, "Now Terah lived seventy years, and begot Abram, Nahor, and Haran," that Abram (also known as Abraham; cf. Genesis 17: 5) was Terah's firstborn, and that he was born when Terah was 70. The truth is, however, **Abraham was not born for another 60 years**. When Stephen was delivering his masterful sermon recorded in Acts 7, he stated that Abraham moved to the land of Palestine "after the death of his father [Terah—EL]" (7:4). Yet if Terah was 205 years old when he died (Genesis 11:32), and Abraham departed Haran when he was 75 (Genesis 12:4), then Terah was 130, not 70, when Abraham was born. In light of this information, John Whitcomb and Henry Morris have aided us in better understanding Genesis 11:26 by paraphrasing it as follows: "And Terah lived seventy years and begat the first of his three sons, the most important of whom (not because of age but because of the Messianic line) was Abram" (1961, p. 480, parenthetical item in orig.).

Lest you think this is an isolated incident (where the son mentioned was not the firstborn son), consider another example. Genesis 5:32 states: "And Noah was five hundred years old, and Noah begot Shem, Ham, and Japheth." Like the situation with Terah begetting Abraham, Nahor, and Haran, here we read that at age 500, Noah begot Shem, Ham, and Japheth. Was Shem the firstborn? Were the three sons of Noah triplets? Or was Shem mentioned first because of his Messianic connection? In all likelihood, the evidence seems to indicate that Shem was not the firstborn, but was born two (or three) years later. Consider the following passages:

> "Noah was six hundred years old when the flood waters were on the earth" (Genesis 7:6).

> "And it came to pass in the **six hundred and first year**, in the first month, the first day of the month, that the waters were dried up from the earth and Noah removed the covering of the ark and looked, and in-

deed the surface of the ground was dry" (Genesis 8:
13, emp. added).

"Shem was **one hundred years** old, and begot Arphaxad **two years after the flood**" (Genesis 11:10,
emp. added).

These verses seem to suggest that Shem was not born when
Noah was 500, but rather when Noah was 502 (or 503 if we
are to understand the phrase "two years after the flood" to mean
when they finally got off the ark and not when the flood waters
ceased coming upon the Earth). A comparison of Genesis 11:
10 with 10:22 may suggest that Shem's son, Arphaxad, was
not the firstborn son in his family. Likely, Shem, Arphaxad,
and others are mentioned first for the same reason Abraham
is–because they are Messianic ancestors, and not because they
were the firstborn sons of their fathers. Interestingly, numerous other Messianic ancestors, such as Seth, Isaac, Jacob, and
Judah, were not firstborn sons. Was Moses being dishonest
when he recorded these genealogies? Absolutely not. We must
remember that

> the year of begetting a first son, known in the Old
> Testament as "the beginning of strength," was an im-
> portant year in the life of the Israelite (Gen. 49:3; Deut.
> 21:17; Psa. 78:51; and Psa. 105:36). It is this year…
> and not the year of the birth of the Messianic link,
> that is given in each case in Genesis 11 (Whitcomb
> and Morris, p. 480).

Just as Genesis 5:32 does not teach that Noah was 500 when
Shem was born, Genesis 11:26 does not teach that Abraham
was born when Terah was 70. This verse basically means that
Terah **began having children** at age 70, not that all three children were born at that age. That Abraham, Nahor, and Haran
were not triplets seems evident from other facts mentioned
throughout Genesis. Considering Nahor's wife was Haran's
daughter (11:29), and Nahor's granddaughter (Rebekah–22:

23; 24:15) married Abraham's son (Isaac—24:67), it is even more clear what Genesis 11:26 means and what it does not mean. Abraham is mentioned first in 11:26 because of his greater importance. It was through his seed that all nations of the Earth would be blessed (12:3; 22:18). Those who allege that Acts 7: 4 contradicts statements found in Genesis 11 and 12 simply are misunderstanding the text by not taking into account that certain Hebrew phrases possess a wider connotation than what might be perceived in modern-day English.

COULD TERAH HAVE BEEN 130 WHEN ABRAHAM WAS BORN?

Genesis 17:17; Acts 7:4

The "problem" with Terah being 130 when Abraham was born has to do with **why** Abraham regarded **his own** ability to beget a son at age 100 as somewhat incredible (Genesis 17: 1,17). Curious and diligent Bible students want to know why the apostle Paul described Abraham's body as being "already dead (since he was about a hundred years old)" [Romans 4: 19; cf. Hebrews 11:12], if **Abraham** was born when his **father** was **130**? Why would Abraham have staggered at the thought of a 100-year-old-man begetting a son—if the above calculations are correct? ["Abraham fell on his face and laughed, and said in his heart, 'Shall a child be born to a man who is one hundred years old?' " (Genesis 17:17).]

First, it should be remembered that Abraham apparently did not think it impossible to sire a child by Hagar at age 85 (Genesis 16). In fact, by insisting that Abraham engage in conjugal relations with her maid, Sarah exhibited confidence in his ability to raise up an heir. In modern times, one only rarely hears of a man in his mid-seventies begetting children. Abraham, on the other hand, begot his **first** son at **86** years of age. Although during Abraham's day the longevity of man was not what it once was (e.g., Noah begot sons at 500 years of age—5: 32), it still was greater than it is today. Thus, we must refrain from comparing the ages of those who sired children thousands of years ago by today's standards.

Another detail often overlooked in Abraham's life is that he had more children than just Ishmael and Isaac. He actually obtained six heirs through a woman he married by the name of Keturah (Genesis 25:1-6; cf. 1 Chronicles 1:32). Because nothing is mentioned about Keturah until after the death of Sarah, it is reasonable to presume that the children she bore to Abraham came along well after Isaac was born. Genesis 23:1-2 states that "Sarah lived one hundred and twenty-seven years" and "died." After reading about Isaac's marriage to Rebekah recorded in Genesis 24, the text says, "Abraham **again** took a wife, and her name was Keturah. And she bore him Zimran, Joktan, Medan, Midian, Ishback, and Shuah" (25:1-2, emp. added). **If** these events are to be understood as occurring in chronological order, it means Abraham was more than 140 when Keturah bore him six sons. [Abraham was ten years older than Sarah (17:17), and thus when Sarah died at 127, Abraham would have been 137. Also, since Isaac was born when Abraham was 100, and he (Isaac) married Rebekah at the age of 40 (25:20), then this would make Abraham at least 140 when he married Keturah.]

It must be admitted, however, that just because the events regarding Abraham's marriage to Keturah are recorded after the death of Sarah, it does not necessarily mean this is the exact order. There are events recorded, and stories told, throughout the Bible that are not written in a chronological format (cf. Genesis 10 and 11; and Matthew 4:1-11 with Luke 4:1-13). As Keil and Delitzch mentioned, "it is not stated anywhere, that Abraham did not take Keturah as his wife till after Sarah's death. It is merely an inference drawn from the fact, that it is not mentioned till afterwards; and it is taken for granted that the history is written in strictly chronological order" (1996). Adam Clarke agreed by stating: "**When** Abraham took Keturah we are not informed; it might have been in the lifetime of Sarah" (1996, emp. added). According to some, "this must have occurred many years before the death of Sarah, for several sons are listed" (*Wycliffe Bible Commentary*, 1962). However, based on the wording of Genesis 25:1, and the fact that neither Keturah nor any of her sons is ever mentioned before this time, it seems more likely that Abraham took Keturah as his wife **after** Sarah died. But, even if it were during his marriage to Sarah, he still would have been close to (if not more than) a century old. Why? Because we read that well after entering the land of Canaan at the age of 75 Abraham was "childless" with "no offspring" (Genesis 15:2-3). Ishmael, Abraham's first child, was not born until he was 86. The "best" scenario (for those who believe Keturah bore Abraham six sons while Sarah was still living) is that Zimran, Joktan, Medan, Midian, Ishback, and Shuah were born sometime after Abraham was 86. Therefore, even the most conservative estimates put Abraham in his nineties during this time—a time when he was still begetting sons.

A final detail that few have considered in light of Abraham's age when Isaac was born, is how old Abraham's grandson, Jacob, was when Joseph was born. According to Genesis 47:9, Jacob was 130 years old when he arrived in Egypt (cf. 47:28), which was at the end of the second year of the famine (45:6,11). Joseph was in his thirtieth year when he stood before Pharaoh nine years earlier at the beginning of the seven years of plenty (41:46). Thus, at the end of the second year of the famine (the year Jacob arrived in Egypt, at the age of 130), Joseph would have been 39 years old. This means that Jacob was 91 when Joseph was born.

If Jacob was 91 when Joseph ("the son of his old age"—37:3) was born, one is curious to know how old he was at the birth of his youngest son, Benjamin. In order to ascertain this figure, one must begin with Jacob's twenty-year commitment to Laban in Padan Aram (Genesis 31:38). The first seven years

Jacob was in Padan Aram serving Laban, he was not married and had no children (29:18-20). After his marriages to Leah and Rachel, the text indicates that all of Jacob's sons, save Benjamin, were born sometime within the next few years (Genesis 29:30-30:25). It was **after** Joseph's birth that Jacob began serving his final six years in Padan Aram (30:25; 31:38,41). We know that Benjamin was more than six years younger than Joseph, because he was not born until sometime after Jacob discontinued working for Laban. Jacob did not receive his twelfth son until after he: (1) departed Padan Aram (31:18); (2) crossed over the river (Euphrates–31:21); (3) met with his brother, Esau, near Penuel (32:22,31; 33:2); (4) built a house in Succoth (33:17); (5) pitched his tent in Shechem (33:18); and (6) built an altar to God at Bethel (35:1-19). Obviously, a considerable amount of time passed between Jacob's separation from Laban in Padan Aram, and the birth of Benjamin near Bethlehem. Biblical commentator Albert Barnes conservatively estimated that Benjamin was 13 years younger than Joseph (1997). Hebrew scholar John T. Willis said Benjamin was likely about 14 years younger than Joseph (1984, p. 433). Actually, if Benjamin were just ten years younger than Joseph (and few, if any, commentators have ever suggested there were less than 10 years between the two), that would mean Jacob was 101 when he begat Benjamin. The fact that Jacob could still beget children when he was 100 years old (with no indication of there being a miracle involved) supports the proposition that Terah, his great-grandfather (who begot Abraham 260 years earlier) could have begotten Abraham at 130 years of age.

The obvious question, then, is why it took a special miracle for Abraham to become a father when he was only 100 years old? Actually, there are several factors that may come into play as to why Abraham was somewhat baffled at the idea of having a child at the age of 100. First, it seems likely that the emphasis of Genesis 17:17 is on the **physical condition** of Abraham at this particular period in his life, and not so much his actual age. It is possible that Abraham simply was failing in health. This would not be surprising, considering his son Isaac experienced a serious failing in health about **44 years** before he (Isaac) died (Genesis 27:1). [NOTE: Since Isaac was 60 years older than Jacob (25:26), and since Jacob was about 91 when Joseph was born (as noted above), Isaac must have been about 151 when Joseph was born. Since Joseph was born after Jacob had been living in Padan Aram for about 14 years, Isaac would have been no more than 137 in Genesis 27:1.] Like Isaac, it may be that Abraham was failing in health at 100, even though he wouldn't die for another 75 years. Considering that his father begot him at 130, and that his grandson sired a child at 100, Abraham's statement about him being 100 years of age when Isaac was promised, likely should be interpreted in light of his physical condition at the time, rather than his actual age.

Even today, men use their age when describing their physical situation. For example, when most 45-year-old men are asked if they could play major league baseball at their current age, they often respond by saying, "I'm too old to play baseball." But does this mean that it can't be done? Obviously not, since Nolan Ryan was still throwing 100-mph fastballs when he was 45. Ricky Henderson was still hitting homeruns and stealing bases at 42 years of age. And at 40 years old, Michael Jordan was still playing professional basketball. Thus, even though we know it still is possible for certain people who are our same age (or older) to do something, we frequently use our age to describe our physical condition. My father begot me when he was 40. However, if someone asks me when I'm 40 if I want any more children, I'll likely respond by saying, "I'm too old to be changing diapers."

It seems clear that the miracle the Almighty worked on Abraham "depended on something else than his mere age" (McGarvey, 1892, p. 118). The miracle was not that He simply made it possible for a 100-year-old man to beget a child (for this was done by others both before and after Abraham begot Isaac), but rather that He miraculously endowed him with new vital and reproductive energy for begetting the son of the promise. As Whitcomb and Morris concluded, "In response to his renewed faith in God and in God's promise (Rom. 4:19), his [Abraham's–EL] body, which was 'now as good as dead,' must have been renewed by God to live out the remaining 75 years and to beget many more children (Gen. 25:1-7)" [1961, p. 480].

Another reason Abraham was so perplexed at the promise of a son (Genesis 17:17) had to do with his wife's physical condition. Genesis 18:11 states: "It had ceased to be with Sarah after the manner of women" (18:11, ASV). Sarah's "periods had ceased with the so-called change of life and with them the capacity to conceive.... Capacity for procreation and conception was extinct" (Luepold, 1942, p. 541). "From the human standpoint, it was impossible for a woman long after the onset of menopause to give birth to a child" (Coffman, 1985b, p. 239). For this reason, J.W. McGarvey, one of the brightest biblical scholars of the nineteenth century, concluded: "The incredulity of Abraham...had reference chiefly to Sarah" (1892, p. 118). Abraham knew it would take a miracle for her to conceive a child (cf. Hebrews 11:11).

A third reason Abraham expressed astonishment upon hearing Jehovah's promise of a son through Sarah could have depended largely on the possibility "that he had now been living thirteen years with a young concubine, Hagar, since the birth of Ishmael, and she had not borne him another son (17: 24,25)" [McGarvey, p. 118]. Although most people would disregard this option because Hagar "became despised" in Sarah's eyes after she conceived Ishmael (16:4), nothing is said about Sarah's feelings toward Hagar for the thirteen years after Hagar gave birth to Ishmael and before Isaac was born. It is more than possible that Abraham continued to "go in to her" during that time. If this was the situation, then certainly Abraham's amazement upon hearing the Lord's promise of a son (Genesis 17:17) could have been due (at least in part) to his inability to beget any more children with Hagar the past thirteen years.

The truth of the matter is that Terah was 130 when Abraham was born. This fact is known because of the inspiration by which Stephen spoke and Luke wrote (Acts 7:4). As renowned New Testament commentator R.C.H. Lenski said, it is a "simple matter of adding a few figures" (1961a, p. 263). It in no way contradicts the statement Moses recorded in Genesis 11:26 (that "Terah lived seventy years, and begot Abram, Nahor, and Haran"), or Abraham's statement in Genesis 17:17. That Abraham thought it incredible for him to have a son at 100 years of age must be understood in light of other information given in Genesis.

- Abraham had been able to "raise up an heir" at the age of 85 (Genesis 16).

- He then had six other sons by Keturah sometime after he was 86 (likely it was "long after" this time; see McGarvey, p. 118).

- Also, Abraham's grandson, Jacob, was 91 when Joseph was born, and approximately 100 when he begot his youngest son, Benjamin.

All of this information leads us to believe that Abraham's amazement at the pronouncement of Isaac at age 100 was due to some other factor than just his being 100 years of age.

- Perhaps the emphasis is more on his **physical condition**, and not so much his actual age (with his age being used to "describe" his failing health).

- Or maybe, as J.W. McGarvey suggested, Abraham expressed amazement because "he had now been living thirteen years with a young concubine, Hagar, since

the birth of Ishmael, and she had not borne him another son (17:24,25)" [p. 118].

* Likely, however, most of Abraham's bewilderment
was due largely to his wife's inability to conceive since
her onset of menopause (18:11).

JESSE'S MISSING SON
1 Samuel 16:11; 17:12; 1 Chronicles 2:13-15

Some time ago, I received a letter from a woman who was
seeking an answer to a question that an unbeliever had presented to her. The question that gave her so much trouble, and
that seemed to plant a seed of doubt in her mind about the inerrancy of Scripture, was this: "Did Jesse (the father of David)
have seven sons or eight?" This question arises from a comparison of the information about Jesse's family in 1 Samuel
16-17, with the genealogy given in 1 Chronicles chapter two.

First Samuel 16 states that Jesse made seven sons pass before the prophet Samuel, in hopes that God would anoint one
of them as the next king of Israel (16:10). Samuel then informed
Jesse that God had not chosen any of these seven sons that
passed before him, but was looking for another. Of course,
that other son was David, "the youngest" (16:11) of Jesse's "eight
sons" (17:12). The "problem" with this information is that the
genealogy in 1 Chronicles 2:13-15 specifically states that David was "the seventh" son of Jesse. How is it that David could
be both the seventh son and eighth son of Jesse? Some are ea-
ger to call this a legitimate Bible contradiction. Even many
Bible students (like the one who wrote me about this question)
read these statements for the first time and wonder if this is an
"inconsistency in the Word." What is the answer? How many
sons did Jesse have? And was David Jesse's eighth son or seventh?

The answer is really quite simple. One of Jesse's sons shown
to Samuel at Bethlehem must have died while young and without posterity. Thus, at one time David was the youngest of **eight**

sons, and at another time he was the youngest of **seven** sons. We must keep in mind that Hebrew genealogies often included only the names of those who had some significance for future generations (see Richards, 1993, p. 106; "Genealogy," 1986). It makes sense that if one of David's brothers died before marrying and begetting children (or before doing something extraordinary), he would not have been mentioned.

Lest you think this situation sounds bizarre, consider the following. Fifty years ago, whenever my father engaged in a discussion about his family, he would tell people that he had **five** brothers and two sisters. Today, when he converses with others about his family he often speaks of his **four** brothers and two sisters. Is he being dishonest when he does so? No. Sadly, when my dad was 19 years old, one of his younger brothers died in a tragic accident. Although this brother was loved deeply and is missed greatly, usually when my father is asked about his siblings he simply says: "I have **four** brothers and two sisters." If he has time or feels there is a need, he then will mention his other brother who died at a very young age. The point is, whether my dad tells someone that he is the oldest of eight children or the oldest of seven children, he is telling the truth.

Admittedly, the Bible does not say specifically that one of David's brothers died at a young age. But, it most likely is implying such a thing when one less son is mentioned in 1 Chronicles 2:13-15. [Considering that David's three oldest brothers were warriors in Saul's army (1 Samuel 17:13ff.), one certainly would not be surprised if one of David's other brothers also became a soldier and died in battle.]

To say that one of David's brothers dying at a relatively young age is not an option is to assert that the Bible does not teach by implication. [Yet, as anyone who has studied the Bible knows, it most certainly does teach by implication (cf. Acts 8:35-36).] Furthermore, if people today who have lost children or siblings can speak legitimately about their family number in two different ways, should we not also give Bible writers the same freedom in their recording of historical families?

WHO WAS JOSEPH'S FATHER?
Matthew 1:16; Luke 3:23

In his book, *The Encyclopedia of Biblical Errancy*, skeptic Dennis McKinsey confidently asserted that the "contradictory" genealogies found in Matthew 1 and Luke 3 open up "a Pandora's box that apologists would just as soon remained closed forever" (1995, p. 46). One "contradiction" he cited (p. 80) revolves around the father of Joseph. Whereas Matthew 1:16 states that "**Jacob begot Joseph** the husband of Mary, of whom was born Jesus who is called Christ" (emp. added), Luke 3:23 says, "Jesus Himself began His ministry at about thirty years of age, being (as was supposed) the son of **Joseph, the son of Heli**" (emp. added). How is it that Joseph could be the son of both Jacob and Heli? Is Mr. McKinsey correct? Do Christian apologists really shudder at the sound of Matthew 1 and Luke 3? Do we cower at the thought of having to explain their differences? Not at all.

The answer to this supposed contradiction is relatively simple: the first seventeen verses in the first chapter of Matthew give the genealogy of Jesus through Joseph, while Luke 3 presents the genealogy of Jesus through Mary. Hence, Jacob is the father of Joseph (Matthew 1:16), while Heli is the father of Mary (Luke 3:23). If this is true, the logical question that both critics and serious Bible students ask is why Mary is not mentioned in Luke's genealogy? The answer is again quite simple: Luke follows the strict Hebrew tradition of mentioning only the names of males. Therefore, in this case, Mary is designated by her husband's name.

Lest you think it is unreasonable to conclude that a son-in-law could be called a son, remember that it is recorded in 1 Samuel 24:16 that King Saul (David's father-in-law—1 Samuel 18:27) called David "son." The term "son" actually has a variety of meanings in the Bible. It can signify: (1) son by actual birth; (2) grandson; (3) descendant; (4) son-in-law; or (5) son by creation, as in the case of Adam (Luke 3:38). All indications are that in Luke 3:23, the phrase "son of Heli" (literally "of Heli") refers to Heli's son-in-law, Joseph. The following evidence clearly supports this rationale.

- The two narrations of the virgin birth are from two different perspectives. Matthew 1:18-25 tells the story only from Joseph's perspective, while Luke 1:26-56 is told wholly from Mary's point of view. It makes sense, then, that Matthew focused on Joseph's lineage in his genealogy, whereas Luke paid careful attention to Mary's ancestors.

- Because the phrase "as was supposed" (Luke 3:23) is used to describe Jesus' relationship with His earthly father, one automatically should see that something is different about this genealogy from the one recorded in Matthew chapter one. The phrase "Jesus...being (**as was supposed**) the son of Joseph" (emp. added) is indicating that He was not really one of Joseph's biological sons, even though the public commonly assumed such.

- Every name in the Greek text of Luke's genealogy, **with the exception of Joseph**, is preceded by the definite article "the" (e.g. the Heli, the Matthat). Although not obvious in our English translations, this stands out to anyone reading the Greek. As nineteenth-century biblical scholar Frederic Godet stated: "The omission of the article puts the name (Joseph) **outside** of the genealogical series" (1890, 1:198, emp. added). In fact, the parentheses in our versions containing the words "(as was supposed)," most likely should be extended to include the name "Joseph"

(Lenski, 1961b, p. 220). [Remember that parentheses have been added in our English Bibles by translators for the sake of "clarity." In this situation, however, it seems translators should have extended the parentheses so that the text reads: "And Jesus Himself began His ministry at about thirty years of age, being **(as was supposed of Joseph)** the son of Heli, the son of Matthat...."] When one's studies take him beyond our English translations into the original language of Scripture (in this case, Greek), he begins to realize all the more that Luke's genealogy is tracing the line of Joseph's wife, even though Joseph's name is used.

These two separate genealogies of Jesus Christ were, in fact, absolutely necessary in the establishment of Christ as the Messiah. The Messianic title, "Son of David," that so frequently was applied to Christ, required dual proof that: (1) He was entitled to the throne, as Matthew's genealogy indicates; and (2) He literally had descended from David, as Luke's genealogy demonstrates. The verses in Matthew clearly establish Christ as the legal heir to the throne by tracing His ancestry down through the royal line of the kings of Israel, with Luke's account demonstrating that He was an actual descendant of David (through Nathan, the brother of Solomon–1 Chronicles 3:5). Jesus literally was born from one of David's virgin "daughters."

WAS CAINAN THE SON OF ARPHAXAD?
Luke 3:36; Genesis 10:24; 11:12; 1 Chronicles 1:18,24

Luke 3:36 is the only verse in the Bible where one can read of the patriarch Arphaxad having a son named Cainan. Although another Cainan (the son of Enosh) is mentioned seven times in Scripture (Genesis 5:9-10,12-14; 1 Chronicles 1:2; Luke 3:37), outside of Luke 3:36, Cainan, the son of Arphaxad, is never mentioned. He is omitted in the genealogies of Genesis 10 and 11, as well as in the genealogy of 1 Chronicles 1:

1-28. When the son of Arphaxad is listed in these genealogies, the name always given is Salah (or Shelah), not Cainan. According to some skeptics, either Cainan's omission from the genealogies in Genesis and First Chronicles represents a genuine mistake, or Luke was in error when he wrote that Arphaxad had a son named Cainan.

One important thing that we learn from the various genealogies throughout Scripture is that sometimes they contain minor gaps–gaps that are both intentional and legitimate. Thus, just because Luke 3 contains a name that is not recorded in Genesis 10 or 11, or in First Chronicles 1, does not necessarily mean that someone made a mistake. The fact is, terms such as "begot," "the son of," and "father"–which often are found in genealogies–occasionally have a much wider connotation in the Bible than might be implied when such words are used in modern-day English. Jacob once called Abraham "father," even though Abraham was really his grandfather (Genesis 32: 9). About 2,000 years later, the Pharisees also referred to Abraham as their "father" (John 8:39). The term "father" in these passages obviously means "ancestor." In the first verse of the New Testament, Matthew wrote of Jesus as being "the son of David, the son of Abraham." Obviously, Matthew knew that Jesus was not an immediate son of either David or Abraham; he simply used these words in the same flexible way that the ancients frequently used them. [Later in his genealogy, Matthew intentionally omitted some other names as well (e.g., Joash, Amaziah, and Azariah; cf. Matthew 1:6-16; 1 Chronicles 3: 11-12). We do not know for sure why Matthew did not include these names in his genealogy (most likely it was for memorization purposes). However, we can be certain that if these gaps represented a legitimate discrepancy, the Jews would have brought it to the attention of Christians 2,000 years ago when they sought to discredit Jesus' royal lineage.]

The simple fact is, just because one genealogy has more (or fewer) names than another genealogy, does not mean that the two genealogies contradict one another. The controversy surrounding Luke 3:36 is readily explainable when one considers the flexibility that the ancients employed in recording the names of "fathers" and "sons."

Still, the insertion of the name Cainan in Luke 3:36 may have a far different explanation—one that (in my mind) is more plausible, yet at the same time is more complicated to explain, and thus less popular. It is my studied conclusion that the "Cainan problem" is the result a scribal error made when copying Luke's gospel account.

Realizing that the New Testament originally was written in Greek without punctuation or spaces between words, the insertion of the name Cainan easily could have crept into Luke's genealogy. Notice what the original text (in agreement with Genesis 10:24, 11:12, and 1 Chronicles 1:18,24) might have said:

touserouchtouragautoufalektouebertousala

toukainamtouarfaxadtouseemtounooetoulamech

*toumathousalatouhenoochtouiarettoumaleleeel**toukainan***

touenoostouseethtouadamtoutheou

If a scribe happened to glance at the end of the third line at **toukainan**, he easily could have written it on the first line as well as the third. Hence, instead of reading of only one Cainan, what we read today is two Cainans:

*touserouchtouragautoufalektouebertousala**toukainan***

toukainamtouarfaxadtouseemtounooetoulamech

*toumathousalatouhenoochtouiarettoumaleleeel**toukainan***

touenoostouseethtouadamtoutheou

As you can see, it would not be difficult for a weary scribe to copy "Cainan" inadvertently from Luke 3:37 as he was copying 3:36 (see Sarfati, 1998, 12[1]:39-40; Morris, 1976, p. 282).

Although some apologists reject the idea that the insertion of Cainan in Luke 3:36 is a copyist's error, the following facts seem to add much credence to this proposed solution.

- As stated earlier, this part of Luke's genealogy also is recorded in Genesis 10:24, 11:12, and in 1 Chronicles 1:18,24. **All** of these Old Testament passages, however, **omit** the Cainan of Luke 3:36. In fact, Cainan, the son of Arphaxad, **is not found in any Hebrew manuscripts of the Old Testament**.
- Cainan is omitted from all of the following ancient versions of the Old Testament: the Samaritan Pentateuch, the Syriac, the Targum (Aramaic translations of the Old Testament), and the Vulgate (a Latin translation of the Bible completed sometime between A.D. 382 and 405) [see Hasel, 1980, pp. 23-37].
- Cainan's name is absent from Flavius Josephus' patriarchal listing in his historical work, *Antiquities of the Jews* (see Book 6, Chapter 1, Sections 4-5).
- The third-century Christian historian, Julius Africanus, also omitted Cainan's name from his chronology of the patriarchs, and yet he had copies of both the gospels of Luke and Matthew (see "Extant Writings...," 1994, pp. 125-140).
- The earliest known copy of Luke (a papyrus codex of the Bodmer Collection dated between A.D. 175 and 225) does not contain this Cainan (see Sarfati, n.d.).

Some are quick to point out that the Septuagint (the Greek translation of the Hebrew Old Testament) mentions the name Cainan, and thus verifies that he was the son of Arphaxad, just as Luke 3:36 indicates. The problem with this line of defense is that the **oldest** Septuagint manuscripts **do not** include this reference to Cainan (Sarfati, 1998, 12[1]:40). Patrick Fairbairn indicated in his Bible encyclopedia that this Cainan does "not appear to have been in the copies of the Septuagint used by Theophilus of Antioch in the second century, by Africanus in the third, or by Eusebius in the fourth" (1957, p. 351). He went on to state that it also was left out of the Vatican copy of the Septuagint (p. 351). That "Cainan" was a later addition to the Septuagint (and not a part of it originally) also is evident from the fact that neither Josephus nor Africanus mentioned him, and yet all indications are that they both used the Septuagint in their writings. [They repeat too many of the same numbers of the Septuagint not to have used it.] Thus, Larry Pierce stated: "It appears that at the time of Josephus, the extra generation of Cainan was not in the LXX [Septuagint—EL] text or the document that Josephus used, otherwise Josephus would have included it!" (1999, 13[2]:76). As Henry Morris concluded in his commentary on Genesis: "[I]t is altogether possible that later copiers of the Septuagint (who were not as meticulous as those who copied the Hebrew text) inserted Cainan into their manuscripts on the basis of certain copies of Luke's Gospel to which they then had access" (1976, p. 282, parenthetical comment in orig.).

Although it may be appropriate to view Luke 3:36 as supplementing the Old Testament genealogies, when all of the evidence is gathered, it appears that the name Cainan in Luke 3:36 was not a part of God's original Word, but is the result of a copyist's error. And as we discussed in the previous chapter, errors made by copyists do not represent legitimate Bible contradictions.

Chapter 9

ALLEGED CONTRADICTIONS SURROUNDING THE RESURRECTION OF JESUS

In his book, *Farewell to God*, Charles Templeton (who worked for years with the Billy Graham Crusade but eventually abandoned his belief in God) used several pages of the book to discuss the comparisons between the statements from the four gospels. He concluded by stating: "The entire resurrection story is not credible" (1996, p. 122). Another well-known preacher-turned-skeptic, Dan Barker, delights in attempting to find contradictions in the different accounts of the resurrection. In his book, *Losing Faith in Faith*, he filled seven pages with a list of "contradictions" among the narratives that he believes he has discovered. Eventually, he stated: "Christians, either tell me exactly what happened on Easter Sunday, or let's leave the Jesus myth buried" (1992, p. 181).

It is interesting, is it not, that Barker demands to know "exactly what happened" on a day in ancient history that occurred almost 2,000 years ago? Such a request speaks loudly of the historical legitimacy of the resurrection story, since no other day in ancient history has ever been examined with such scrutiny. Historians today cannot tell "exactly what happened" on July 4, 1776 or April 12, 1861, yet Christians are expected to provide the "exact" details of Christ's resurrection? Fortunately, the gospel writers described "exactly what happened"–without contradiction. Examine the evidence.

HEAD-ON COLLUSION

"Collusion: A secret agreement between two or more parties for a fraudulent, illegal, or deceitful purpose" (*The American Heritage Dictionary of the English Language*, 2000, p. 363). Even if we have not heard the word "collusion" before, most of us understand the situation it describes. Suppose four bank robbers don their nylon-hose masks, rob the city bank, stash the cash in a nearby cave, and then each goes back to his respective house until the police search is concluded. The first robber hears a knock on his door and upon opening it finds a policeman who "just wants to ask him a few questions." The officer asks, "Where were you and what where you doing on the night of January 2, 2003?" The thief promptly answers, "I was at Joe Johnson's house watching television with three other friends." The policeman gets the three friends' names and addresses and visits each one of their homes. Every robber tells the exact same story. Was it true? Absolutely not! But did the stories all sound exactly the same, with seemingly no contradictions? Yes.

Now, let's examine this principle in light of our discussion of the resurrection. If every single narrative describing the resurrection sounded exactly the same, what do you think would be said about the narratives? "They must have copied each other!" In fact, in other areas of Christ's life besides the resurrection, when the books of Matthew and Luke give the same information as the book of Mark, many people today claim that they must have copied Mark because it is thought to be the earliest of the three books. Another raging question in today's upper echelons of biblical "scholarship" is whether Peter copied Jude in 2 Peter 2:4-17 (or whether Jude copied Peter), because the two segments of Scripture sound so similar. In commenting on alleged contradictions in the gospel accounts, R.C. Foster made this cogent point:

> For years critics have declared that these accounts are hopelessly in contradiction and cannot be harmonized. By their own argument, then, the accounts certainly cannot have been copied from one another. While the differences can be harmonized, no conceivable explanation can be offered as to how such differences could have arisen, if the narratives were copied from one another or from a common source. If the narratives were written independently by eyewitnesses or upon the testimony of eyewitnesses, then such variations are the natural result of independent narration; but, if the narratives were copied from one another, what writers could have been so stupid or perverse as deliberately to have changed the record thus? (1971, pp. 1043-1044).

Clearly, the Bible has not left the prospect of collusion open to the resurrection narratives. It cannot be denied (legitimately) that the resurrection accounts obviously have come to us from **independent** sources. In his book, *Science Versus Religion*, Tad S. Clements vigorously denied that there is enough evidence to justify a personal belief in the resurrection. However, Clements did acknowledge: "There isn't merely one account of Christ's resurrection but rather an embarrassing multitude of stories…" (1990, p. 193). While he opined that these stories "disagree in significant respects," he nevertheless made it clear that the gospels **are** separate accounts of the same story. Dan Barker admitted the same when he boldly stated: "Since

Easter [his wording for the resurrection account–EL] is told by five different writers, it gives one of the best chances to confirm or disconfirm the account" (1992, p. 179). One door that everyone on either side of the resurrection discussion admits has been locked forever by the gospel accounts is the deadbolted door of collusion.

ADDITION DOES NOT A CONTRADICTION MAKE

Suppose I told you that in 1994 I tore the anterior cruciate ligament in my **left knee** while playing basketball in high school. But then, later, when you were visiting with my mother, she informed you that I tore the anterior cruciate ligament in my **right knee** while playing basketball in 1994. Is there a contradiction because I told you I injured my left knee, while my mother mentioned that I hurt my right knee? Not at all. She simply added to (or supplemented) the story I told in order to make the story more complete. (The truth is I tore ligaments in both knees in the same year.) The addition or exclusion of information by two or more individuals does not mean the two testimonies are contradictory. (For more discussion on this point, refer back to chapter one.) Such variation is observed in the lecture notes taken by college students in the same classroom: some simply take more copious notes than others. But that does not mean they are not all equally valid witnesses to what their instructor said. If one student recorded that Abraham Lincoln delivered his famous Gettysburg Address "in November of 1863 to honor those who died in the Civil War Battle of Gettysburg," and another student wrote that the speech was delivered "on November 19, 1863 in Gettysburg, Pennsylvania," their notes would not be considered contradictory, but supplementary. Similarly, what we find throughout the resurrection accounts are additions that make the story more complete.

WHO WERE THE WOMEN?
Matthew 28:1; Mark 16:1; Luke 24:10; John 20:1

The gospel of Matthew names "Mary Magdalene and the other Mary" as women who visited Christ's tomb early on the first day of the week (28:1). Mark cites Mary Magdalene, Mary the mother of James, and Salome as the callers (16:1). Luke mentions Mary Magdalene, Joanna, Mary the mother of James, and "the other women" (24:10). Yet John talks only about Mary Magdalene visiting the tomb early on Sunday (20:1). Dan Barker cited these different names as discrepancies and contradictions on page 182 of his book. But do these different lists truly contradict one another? No, they do not. They are supplementary (with each writer adding names to make the list more complete), not contradictory. If John had said "**only** Mary Magdalene visited the tomb," or if Matthew had stated that "Mary Magdalene and the other Mary were the **only** women to visit the tomb," then there would be a contradiction. As it stands, no contradiction occurs. To further illustrate this point, suppose that you have 10 one-dollar bills in your pocket. Someone comes up to you and asks, "Do you have a dollar bill in your pocket?" Naturally, you respond in the affirmative. Suppose another person asks, "Do you have five dollars in your pocket?," and again you say that you do. Finally, another person asks, "Do you have ten dollars in your pocket?," and you say yes for the third time. Did you tell the truth every time? Yes. Were any of your answers contradictory? No. Were all three statements about the contents of your pockets different? Yes. Supplementation does not equal contradiction.

WHO WAS AT THE TOMB?
Matthew 28:2-5; Mark 16:5; Luke 24:4; John 20:12

Also fitting into the discussion of supplementation are the angels, men, and young man described in the different resurrection accounts. Two "problems" arise with the entrance of the "holy heralds" at the empty tomb of Christ. First, how many were there? Second, were they angels or men? The account in Matthew cites "an angel of the Lord who descended from heaven" and whose "appearance was as lightning, and his raiment white as snow" (28:2-5). Mark's account presents a slightly different picture of "a young man sitting on the right side, arrayed in a white robe" (16:5). But Luke mentions "two men stood by them [the women–EL] in dazzling apparel" (24:4). And, finally, John writes about "two angels in white sitting, one at the head, and one at the feet, where the body of Jesus had lain" (20:12). Are any of these accounts contradictory as to the **number** of men or angels at the tomb? Factoring in the supplementation rule, we must answer in the negative. Although the accounts are different, they are not contradictory as to the number of messengers. Mark does not mention "**only** a young man" and Luke does not say there were "**exactly** two angels." Was there one messenger at the tomb? Yes. Were there two as well? Yes. Once again, supplementation does not equal contradiction.

Our second question concerning the messengers is their identity: **Were they angels or men**? Most people who are familiar with the Old Testament have no problem answering this question. Genesis chapters 18 and 19 mention three "men" who came to visit Abraham and Sarah. These men stayed for a short time, and then two of them continued on to visit the city of Sodom. The Bible tells us in Genesis 19:1 that these "men" were actually angels. Yet when the men of Sodom came to do violence to these angels, the city dwellers asked: "Where are the **men** that came in to thee this night?" (Genesis 19:5). Throughout the two chapters, the messengers are referred to as both men and angels with equal accuracy. They looked like, talked like, walked like, and sounded like men. Could they then be referred to (legitimately) as men? Yes. But were they angels? Yes.

To illustrate, suppose you saw a man sit down at a park bench and take off his right shoe. As you watched, he began to pull out an antenna from the toe of the shoe and a number pad from the heel. He proceeded to dial a number and began to talk to someone over his "shoe phone." If you were going to write down what you saw, could you accurately say that the man dialed a number on his shoe? Yes. Could you say that he dialed a number on his phone? Indeed you could. The shoe had heel, a sole, a toe, and everything else germane to a shoe, but it was much more than a shoe. In the same way, the messengers at the tomb could be described accurately as men—they had a head perched on two shoulders and held in place by a neck, and they had a body complete with arms and legs, etc. So, they were men. But, in truth, they were much more than men because they were angels—holy messengers sent from God's thrown to deliver an announcement to certain people. Taking into account the fact that the Old Testament often uses the term "men" to describe angels who have assumed a human form, it is fairly easy to show that no contradiction exists concerning the identity of the messengers.

WHAT TIME DID THE WOMEN VISIT THE TOMB?

Matthew 28:1; Mark 16:2; Luke 24:1; John 20:1

Some Bible critics demand that the time of day at which the women visited the empty tomb of Jesus is different when the gospel of John is compared with the other three accounts. Please read for yourself the four different accounts that follow (emphasis has been added to underscore the time of day under discussion).

> Matthew 28:1: "Now after the Sabbath, as the first day of the week **began to dawn**, Mary Magdalene and the other Mary came to see the tomb."

Mark 16:2: **"Very early in the morning**, on the first day of the week, they came to the tomb **when the sun had risen**."

Luke 24:1: "Now on the first day of the week, **very early in the morning**, they, and certain other women with them, came to the tomb...."

John 20:1: "Now the first day of the week Mary Magdalene went to the tomb **early, while it was still dark**...."

If these four accounts were in any ancient book other than the Bible, they hardly would be questioned as contradictory. In fact, they most likely would be considered to be in perfect agreement. Yet the Bible often is scrutinized much more strictly than any other book that records ancient history. If the above accounts were read to a group of third graders, could they understand what time of day was under discussion? To ask is to answer. Everyone who reads the accounts can see quite plainly that the women visited the tomb sometime very early on the first day of the week while the light was yet struggling with darkness. It is not difficult to understand how Mary Magdalene could have arrived at the tomb while it was yet dark, **and** as it began to dawn, **and** at early dawn. The fact is, it was so early in the morning that the Sun had not fully come up, and thus a hint of darkness lingered over the scene.

DID JESUS HAVE THE SAME PHYSICAL BODY AFTER HIS RESURRECTION?
Luke 24:37; John 20:10-16; Luke 24:39; John 20:27

A gentleman once e-mailed our offices at Apologetics Press, questioning whether Jesus had the same body after His resurrection as He did before being raised from the grave. According to this man, Jesus "appeared to people He knew but nobody recognized Him.... It's as though He had a different body" –and possibly one that was not physical.

At the outset, it is incorrect to assert that "nobody recognized Him," because Matthew 28:9,17 clearly implies that at least some of Jesus' disciples knew Who He was and worshipped Him. Moreover, that Jesus had essentially the same physical body after His resurrection that He had when He died on the cross is evident from at least three different passages. In Luke 24:39, Jesus stated: "Behold My hands and My feet, that it is I Myself. Handle Me and see, for a spirit does not have flesh and bones as you see I have." Jesus expected His disciples to observe **His physical** body. Later in the same chapter, we read that Jesus ate a meal with His disciples (24:42-43; cf. Acts 10:41). And then in John 20:25-29, which is the most frequently cited passage in defense of Christ's having His same physical body, Thomas touched Jesus' nail-scared hands and reached into His side that had been pierced with the Roman spear.

But what about those occasions when some of His disciples did not recognize Him? Do such verses as Luke 24:31,37 and John 20:10-16 represent a contradictory element in the resurrection story? First, just because the text says that the disciples thought they had seen a spirit when they actually saw Jesus (Luke 24:37), does not indicate that He looked different. Since they knew He had been killed, seeing His resurrected body caused them to think that He was in spirit form rather than physical. On one occasion, before Jesus was ever crucified and raised from the grave, His disciples were startled at His appearance, supposing He was a ghost (Mark 6:49). A similar thing happened to Peter when some thought his unexpected presence must be an indication that "it is his angel" (Acts 12:15).

Second, the reason the two disciples who were traveling on the road to Emmaus failed to recognize Jesus initially was not because Jesus had a different body, but because God had miraculously prevented them from recognizing Him. Luke 24:16 indicates that at the beginning of their conversation with

Jesus "their eyes were restrained," but then just before Jesus vanished from their sight, "their eyes were opened and they knew Him" (24:31). Thus, the disciples' recognition ability failed, not because Jesus possessed a different body, but because their eyes were miraculously restrained.

A final person often mentioned as not having recognized the Savior (allegedly because Jesus had a different body) is Mary Magdalene. John 20:11-18 certainly testifies of her initial inability to identify Jesus. The question is: Was Mary's failure to recognize Jesus **her** fault, or the result of Jesus having a different body? As with the above cases, there is no indication in John 20:11-18 that Jesus had anything other than His risen crucified body (cf. 20:25-29). There are at least four possibilities, however, as to why Mary failed to recognize Jesus right at first.

- The Sun may not have risen all the way yet, thus making it difficult to see (cf. 20:1).

- Mary was engaged in deep weeping that likely obscured her vision (20:11,13). In fact, the first words Jesus said to Mary were, "Woman, why are you weeping?" (vs. 15).

- Considering Jesus' clothes were taken from Him when He was crucified (John 19:23-24), and that the linen cloths which were used in His burial were lying in the tomb (John 20:6-7), Jesus likely was wearing clothes that made His exact identity less conspicuous at first glance. Perhaps His post-resurrection attire was similar to what a gardener or watchman would wear (cf. John 20:15).

- It also is possible that Mary's eyes were restrained miraculously, as were the disciples with whom Jesus conversed on the road to Emmaus.

Once all of the Scriptures are taken in to account, one can
see clearly that Jesus physically rose from the grave in essentially the same body that was crucified on the cross. The fact
that some of Jesus' disciples did not immediately recognize
Him, in no way contradicts His physical resurrection.

WAS THE TOMB OPEN WHEN
THE WOMEN ARRIVED?

Matthew 28:2; Mark 16:4; Luke 24:2; John 20:1

According to Mark, Luke, and John, by the time Mary Magdalene and the other women reached the sepulcher of Jesus
on the first day of the week after Christ's crucifixion, the great
stone covering the entrance to His tomb already had rolled
away (16:4; 24:2; 20:1). Matthew, on the other hand, mentions the rolling away of the stone **after** writing that the women
"came to see the tomb." In fact, at first glance it seems that
Matthew 28:1-6 indicates several significant things took place
in the presence of the women.

> Now after the Sabbath, as the first day of the week
> began to dawn, Mary Magdalene and the other Mary
> came to see the tomb. And behold, there was a great
> earthquake; for an angel of the Lord descended from
> heaven, and came and rolled back the stone from the
> door, and sat on it. His countenance was like light-
> ning, and his clothing as white as snow. And the guards
> shook for fear of him, and became like dead men.
> But the angel answered and said to the women, "Do
> not be afraid, for I know that you seek Jesus who was
> crucified. He is not here; for He is risen, as He said.
> Come, see the place where the Lord lay."

How is this passage explained in light of the fact that the other
gospel writers clearly affirmed that the great stone blocking
the entrance to the tomb had rolled away **before** the women
arrived?

The explanation to this "problem" is that the events recorded in Matthew 28:1-6 were not written chronologically. Matthew did not intend for his readers to conclude from this section of Scripture that the women actually saw the stone roll away from the door of Jesus' sepulcher. On the contrary, verse 6 implies "Christ was already risen; and therefore the earthquake and its accompaniments must have taken place at an earlier point of time, to which the sacred writer returns back in his narration" (Robinson, 1993, p. 17). Verses 2-4 serve more as a footnote to the reader (explaining events that took place prior to the women's arrival), and are in no way an indication that Matthew believed the women arrived at the tomb while it still was closed.

The simple fact is, Bible writers did not always record information in a strictly chronological sequence. The first book of the Bible contains several examples where events are recorded more topically than chronologically. Genesis 2:5-25 does not pick up where Genesis 1 left off; rather, it provides more detailed information about some of the events mentioned in chapter one. Some of the things recorded in Genesis 10 occurred after the incident involving the Tower of Babel (recorded in chapter 11). And a number of the events in Genesis 38 involving Judah and Tamar occurred while the things recorded in chapters 39ff. took place. Similar to a teacher who is telling her class a story, and inserts information into it about something the main character did in the past or will do in the future, Bible writers occasionally "jump" ahead of themselves by inserting pertinent parenthetical material.

As a person studies the narrative technique of Matthew (and other Bible writers), he quickly realizes that the writer of the first gospel sometimes arranged his account in **topical** order rather than in a strictly **chronological** order. Matthew 28:1-6 is just one example. Another example can be found in Matthew 21:12-22. Whereas Matthew recorded the cleansing of the temple before Jesus cursed the fig tree (21:12-19), Mark placed the temple cleansing after Jesus cursed the tree (11:15-19). When comparing the two gospel accounts, one soon finds that Matthew's narrative is more of a summary, while Mark's account is more detailed and orderly. Christ actually made two trips to the temple (Mark 11:11,15), and cursed the fig tree on His second trip. Mark reveals that Jesus did not cleanse the temple on the day of his triumphal entry into the city, but on the day following. Matthew, on the other hand, takes the more topical approach and addresses the two trips of Christ to the temple as though they were one event. The same is true of the events recorded in Matthew 28:1-6. What Mark, Luke, and John state more particularly, and have "divided," Matthew mentions together.

PERSPECTIVE PLAYS A PART

What we continue to see in the independent resurrection narratives is not contradiction, but merely differences in perspective. Suppose a man had a 4x6 index card that was solid red on one side and solid white on the other. Further suppose that he stood in front of a large crowd, asked all the men to close their eyes, showed the women in the audience the red side of the card, and then had them write down what they saw. Further suppose that he had all the women close their eyes while he showed the men the white side of the card and had them write down what they saw. One group saw a red card and one group saw a white card. When their answers are compared, it would look at first like they were contradictory, yet they were not. The reason the descriptions appeared contradictory was because the two groups had a different perspective, since each had seen a different side of the same card.

The perspective phenomenon plays a big part in everyday life. In the same way that no two witnesses ever see a car accident in exactly the same way, none of the witnesses of the resurrected Jesus saw the events from the same angle as the others. They are independent narratives. But they do harmonize.

Chapter 10

MISCELLANEOUS ALLEGED CONTRADICTIONS

ISHMAELITES OR MIDIANITES?

Genesis 37:27,36; 39:1

While enjoying a meal and listening to their brother Joseph cry out from the pit into which they had cast him, the sons of Jacob (minus Reuben) noticed a group of merchants coming from Gilead. Rather than killing Joseph and concealing his body, the band of brothers chose to "sell him to the Ishmael-ites" (Genesis 37:27). The Ishmaelites, in turn, took Joseph down to Egypt and sold him to Potiphar, an officer of Pharaoh and captain of the guard (39:1). Skeptics charge that the author of Genesis erred when writing about the details of Joseph being sold into slavery. They insist that a clear contradiction exists because Genesis 37:36 says that "the **Midianites**" sold Joseph "in Egypt to Potiphar, an officer of Pharaoh and captain of the guard" (emp. added), whereas Genesis 39:1 indicates that Joseph was sold to Potiphar by the **Ishmaelites**.

The casual reader of the Bible might be troubled by the different names given in Genesis 37:36 and 39:1. After a thorough study of the Scriptures, however, one can easily see that the names "Ishmaelites" and "Midianites" are used interchangeably. The book of Judges records that after Gideon and his 300 mighty men defeated their enemy,

> [t]he men of Israel said to Gideon, "Rule over us, both you and your son, and your grandson also; for you have delivered us from **the hand of Midian**...." Then Gideon said to them, "I would like to make a request of you, that each of you would give me the earrings from his plunder." For they [those whom Gideon and his men had just conquered—EL] had gold earrings, because **they were Ishmaelites**.... Now the weight of the gold earrings that he requested was one thousand seven hundred shekels of gold, besides the crescent ornaments, pendants, and purple robes which were on **the kings of Midian** (Judges 8:22,24,26, emp. added).

After Gideon had delivered the Israelites from the hand of Midian, he requested the golden earrings that the Israelites had plundered. Plundered from whom? From those whom Gideon and the Israelites had just conquered. And who were they? Like Moses, in his inspired historical narrative concerning Joseph, the inspired writer of Judges referred to the people of Midian as Ishmaelites.

The Midianites and Ishmaelites mentioned in Genesis chapters 37 and 39 were the same group of traders. This is not a contradiction; nor is it proof that Genesis was written by different authors. As Keil and Delitzch concluded:

> The different names given to the traders...do not show that the account has been drawn from different legends, but that these tribes were often confounded, from the fact that they resembled one another so closely,

not only in their common descent from Abraham (Gen. 16:15 and 25:2), but also in the similarity of their mode of life and their constant change of abode, that strangers could hardly distinguish them, especially when they appeared not as tribes but as Arabian merchants, such as they are here described as being (1996).

WHO WROTE ON THE SECOND PAIR OF TABLETS?

Exodus 34:27-28; Deuteronomy 10:1-4

After Moses broke the first tablets of stone that the Lord gave him on Mount Sinai, God commanded him to cut out two tablets of stone (like the first ones) and present himself to Him at the top of Mount Sinai—again (Exodus 34:1-2). Skeptics claim the Bible teaches in Exodus 34 that Moses wrote on this second pair of tablets, whereas in Deuteronomy 10 it says that God is the One Who wrote on these tablets. Based upon this "difference," they allege that a blatant contradiction exists. A closer examination of these passages, however, reveals that they are not contradictory, but rather complementary and consistent with each other.

We readily admit that Deuteronomy 10 teaches that God was the One Who wrote on the second pair of tablets. Verses 1-4 of that chapter say:

> At that time the Lord said to me [Moses], "Hew for yourself two tablets of stone like the first, and come up to Me on the mountain and make yourself an ark of wood. And **I** [God] **will write on the tablets** the words that were on the first tablets, which you broke; and you shall put them in the ark." So I [Moses] made an ark of acacia wood, hewed two tablets of stone like the first, and went up the mountain, having the two tablets in my hand. And **He** [God] **wrote on the tablets** according to the first writing, the Ten Commandments, which the Lord had spoken to you in the moun-

tain from the midst of the fire in the day of the assembly; and the Lord gave them to me (emp. and bracketed items added).

This passage teaches that Moses hewed the tablets out of rock, but that God was the One Who wrote on them. Skeptics agree.

The controversial passage found in Exodus 34 states: "Then the Lord said to Moses, 'Write these words, for according to the tenor of these words I have made a covenant with you and with Israel.' So he was there with the Lord forty days and forty nights; he neither ate bread nor drank water. And **He** wrote on the tablets the words of the covenant, the Ten Commandments" (34:27-28, emp. added). Based upon this passage, critics of the Bible's inerrancy suggest that Moses, not God, wrote on the second pair of tablets. Thus they conclude that Exodus 34 and Deuteronomy 10 contradict one another.

Admittedly, at first glance it seems these verses teach that: (1) Moses was commanded to write the words on the second pair of tablets; and (2) after he was commanded to do so, he (Moses) actually "wrote on the tablets the words of the covenant." But what may seem to be the correct interpretation of a passage is sometimes not the case, especially when the context of the passage is ignored. The words that God instructed Moses to write were "these words," which He had spoken in the preceding verses (i.e., 34:10-26–the ceremonial and judicial injunctions, not the ten "words" of Exodus 20:2-17). The re-writing of the Ten Commandments on the newly prepared slabs was done by God's own hand. God specifically stated in the first verse of Exodus 34 that He (not Moses) would write the same words that had been written on the first tablets of stone that Moses broke. In verse 28 of that chapter, we have it on record that God did what He said He would do in verse one (cf. Deuteronomy 10:2-4). The only thing verse 27 teaches is that Moses wrote the list of regulations given in verses 10-26. That these regulations were not the Ten Commandments is obvious in that there are not even ten of them listed (Coffman, 1985a, p. 474).

Contrary to what skeptics allege, Exodus 34 and Deuteronomy 10 are not contradictory. Moses was not acting under divine direction to physically write the Decalogue on the second pair of tablets. Rather, as Jamieson, Fausset, and Brown recognized in their commentary on Deuteronomy, "God Himself…made the inscription a second time with His own hand, to testify of the importance He attached to the Ten Commandments" (1997).

WHO KILLED KING SAUL?
1 Samuel 31:4; 2 Samuel 1:10; 21:12

Was Saul killed by a Philistine, an Amalakite, or did he kill himself? The context for the statement in 2 Samuel 21:12 can be found one book earlier in 1 Samuel 31, which centers on the fact that the Israelites and the Philistines were engaged in an important battle against each other. First Samuel 31:1 indicates that "the Philistines fought against Israel; and the men of Israel fled from before the Philistines, and fell slain on mount Gilboa." From this simple commentary by the writer, it is clear that the battle was not going well for God's people. Israel's finest-trained armies had been thoroughly and completely routed. Her battle-weary soldiers not only were in disarray, but full retreat. Even their king, Saul, was in peril. In fact, the next two verses go on to explain: "Then the Philistines followed hard after Saul and his sons. And the Philistines killed Jonathan, Abinadab, and Malchishua, Saul's sons. The battle became fierce against Saul. The archers hit him, and he was severely wounded by the archers."

Israel's first king was mortally wounded by the Philistines' arrows. Knowing he was in his death throes, Saul determined not to fall into the hands of his enemies while still living. He therefore turned to his armorbearer and said: "Draw your sword, and thrust me through with it, lest these uncircumcised

men come and thrust me through and abuse me" (31:4a). Verses
4-6 present the conclusion of the matter: "But his armorbearer
would not, for he was greatly afraid. Therefore Saul took a
sword and fell on it. And when his armorbearer saw that Saul
was dead, he also fell on his sword, and died with him. So Saul,
his three sons, his armorbearer, and all his men died together
that same day."

So how did Saul die? Did "a Philistine" kill him? Or did
Saul commit suicide to escape capture and possible torture at
the hands of some of his most feared enemies, as 1 Samuel
31:4 seems to indicate?

The Philistines (as they battled against the Israelites) ulti-
mately were responsible for Saul's self-inflicted wound and
subsequent death. If a modern-day soldier were in the same
situation, wounded by an enemy's bullet, he might take his
own life on the battlefield to avoid capture and torture. Were
a journalist to write an article for a national or local newspaper, might he not (justifiably) report that the soldier died at
the hands of his enemy as a direct result of the battle? Indeed
he might, for had the events never unfolded as they did, obviously the soldier would not have died under such circumstances.

But if the reporter continued his story in the next day's edition of that same newspaper, and, in giving additional details
of the circumstances surrounding the battle, went on to state
that the young man had taken his own life rather than fall into
the enemy's possession and possibly become a tool of betrayal
against his comrades, would any reader of the two-part account
suggest that the journalist had "contradicted" himself? Hardly.
The normal reader, with average common sense, would recognize that in the **general** context, the enemy had caused the
young soldier's death. In the **immediate** context, his death
had been at his own hand as a direct result of his fear of being
captured by that enemy.

The circumstances surrounding Saul's death were no different. The writer of 2 Samuel 21 was correct, in the **general** context, in assigning Saul's demise to "the Philistines," because it was in the battle with the Philistines that Saul found himself dying of wounds caused by their arrows, and thus committed suicide. The writer of 1 Samuel 31:4 was correct, in the **immediate** context, in providing additional information regarding exactly **how** that death occurred—i.e., at Saul's own hand as he lay mortally wounded and in danger of capture and torture.

But what about the story that is recorded in 2 Samuel 1:1-16, wherein an Amalekite claimed to have killed the Israelite's beloved king? The context of this story is as follows. David had just returned from a battle with the Amalekites. While in the city of Ziklag, a young man in ragged clothing appeared before him with a report of Saul's death. The young man, himself an Amalekite, stated:

> "As I happened by chance to be on Mount Gilboa, there was Saul, leaning on his spear; and indeed the chariots and horsemen followed hard after him. Now when he looked behind him, he saw me and called to me. And I answered, 'Here I am.' And he said to me, 'Who are you?' So I answered him, 'I am an Amalekite.' He said to me again, 'Please stand over me and kill me, for anguish has come upon me, but my life still remains in me.' **So I stood over him and killed him**, because I was sure that he could not live after he had fallen. And I took the crown that was on his head and the bracelet that was on his arm, and have brought them here to my lord" (2 Samuel 1:6-10, emp. added).

David's response to this story was one of outrage. At hearing the young man's report, he inquired: "How was it you were not afraid to put forth your hand to destroy the Lord's anointed?"

(2 Samuel 1:14). Turning to the Amalekite, he sternly said: "Your blood is on your own head, for your own mouth has testified against you, saying, 'I have killed the Lord's anointed.'" David then ordered one of his own soldiers to slay the young man as punishment for the atrocity he claimed to have committed—the murder of Israel's king, Saul (2 Samuel 1:15-16).

How can this story be reconciled with the accounts in 1 Samuel 31 and 2 Samuel 21? Isolated from both the general and immediate historical context, the simple fact is that it cannot. Is this, then, an unavoidable, unexplainable contradiction as skeptics allege? No, it is not. Actually, the Amalekite's story is not presented as being the truth of what happened on the battlefield during Saul's dying moments; it is only a record of what the Amalekite **said** had taken place. Gleason Archer made the following observation of this passage:

> Coming with Saul's crown and bracelet in hand and presenting them before the new king of Israel, the Amalekite obviously expected a handsome reward and high preferment in the service of Saul's successor. In the light of the straightforward account in the previous chapter, we must conclude that the Amalekite was lying in order to gain a cordial welcome from David. But what had actually happened was that after Saul had killed himself, and the armorbearer had followed his lord's example by taking his own life (1 Sam. 31:5), the Amalekite happened by at that moment, recognized the king's corpse, and quickly stripped off the bracelet and crown before the Philistine troops discovered it. Capitalizing on his good fortune, the Amalekite then escaped from the bloody field and made his way down to David's headquarters in Ziklag. But his hoped-for reward turned out to be a warrant for his death; David had him killed on the spot.... His glib falsehood had brought him the very opposite of what he had expected, for he failed to foresee

that David's high code of honor would lead him to
make just the response he did (1982, pp. 181-182, emp.
added).

It would not be unusual for a Bible writer to record a story
that was told at the time as the truth, when, in fact, it was a lie.
Moses recorded Satan's lie to Eve in Genesis 3:4, without comment on its false nature. The writer of 1 Kings 13 recorded the
lie of the older prophet to the younger prophet (a lie that ulti-
mately caused the younger prophet's death). John recorded
Peter's three-fold lie when he denied being one of Christ's disciples (18:15-27). Other similar examples could be offered. The
point is, just because the Amalekite mercenary **claimed** to
have killed King Saul does not mean that he was telling the
truth when he made such a claim. In fact, we know he was not
because elsewhere (e.g., 1 Samuel 31:4-5) the actual facts of
the case are presented with great clarity. Once again, the skeptic's claim of a biblical discrepancy can be answered by a common-sense appeal to reason that provides a solution consistent
with the available facts.

MOTIVES MATTER
2 Kings 10:30; Hosea 1:4

In roughly 841 B.C., the commander of Israel's army, Jehu
the son of Jehoshaphat, was anointed king over the northern
kingdom, and was instructed by the Lord to "strike down the
house of Ahab" and "cut off from Ahab all the males in Israel,
both bond and free" (2 Kings 9:6-10). After receiving this command from the Lord via one of "the sons of the prophets," Jehu
began his assassination of Ahab's family. He started by slay-
ing Ahab's son, Joram (also known as Jehoram), who was ruling Israel at the time Jehu was anointed king. He then proceeded
to kill Ahaziah (the king of Judah and grandson of Jezebel–9:
27-29) and forty-two of Ahaziah's brethren (10:12-14). Later,
he slew (or had others slay) Jezebel (the mother of Joram and
former wife of the deceased Ahab–9:30-37), all seventy sons

of Ahab who were living in Samaria, and "all who remained to Ahab in Samaria" (10:1-10,17), and "all who remained of the house of Ahab in Jezreel," including "all his great men and his close acquaintances, and his priests" (10:11). Jehu's final stop was at the temple of Baal where, upon gathering all the Baal-worshipping leaders of Israel into the temple, he locked them up and had them massacred (10:18-27).

After Jehu had carried out his orders to obliterate all males from the house of Ahab, the Lord said to him, "Because you have done well in doing what is right in My sight, and have done to the house of Ahab all that was in My heart, your sons shall sit on the throne of Israel to the fourth generation" (10:30). Jehu had taken the most thorough means of suppressing the idolatry in Israel, and thus was granted protection on his throne, along with his sons after him unto "the fourth generation." The following chapters of 2 Kings indicate that the Lord was true to His word (as always; cf. Titus 1:2). Although the reigns of Jehu's sons were described as kings who "did evil in the sight of Yahweh," the Lord allowed them to reign to the fourth generation in order to fulfill His promise to Jehu.

Several years after the above events took place, the prophet Hosea expressed words that many skeptics have claimed are in opposition to what is stated in 2 Kings 9-10. When Gomer, Hosea's wife, bore a son, Hosea declared that the Lord said, "Call his name Jezreel, for in a little while I will avenge the bloodshed of Jezreel on the house of Jehu, and bring an end to the kingdom of the house of Israel" (1:4). Those trying to discredit the Bible's integrity argue that Hosea put himself into **obvious disagreement** with the inspired writer of 2 Kings, who thought that Jehu had done "all" that was in God's heart. Skeptics claim that the author of 2 Kings heaped praise on Jehu for the Jezreel massacre, but Hosea contradicted him when he said that Lord would avenge the blood of Jezreel and end the reign of the house of Jehu in Israel.

What can be said about this "obvious disagreement"? Are these two passages harmonious, or is this a legitimate contradiction that should cause all Bible believers to reject the book that has been tried and tested for hundreds of years?

First, we cannot be 100% certain that Hosea 1:4 is referring to the events in 2 Kings 9-10. Although nearly all skeptics and Bible commentators link the two passages together, it must be understood that just because 2 Kings 9-10 is the only place in the Old Testament that describes suitable events located at Jezreel, it does not mean that Hosea **must** have been referring to those events. The honest student of God's Word has to admit that Hosea may have been referring to Jehu's sons who reigned after him. Perhaps his sons performed serious atrocities in Jezreel that are not recorded in 2 Kings. One cannot be certain that Hosea was indeed referring to the events recorded in 2 Kings 10. Having made such a disclaimer, it is my position that these two passages **should** be linked together, and thus the alleged contradiction skeptics raise deserves an adequate explanation: How could God instruct Jehu to destroy the house of Ahab, and then later condemn him (his house) through the words of Hosea for having done so?

The answer really is quite simple. As Norman Geisler and Thomas Howe observed: "God praised Jehu for obeying Him in destroying the house of Ahab, but condemned Jehu for his sinful motive in shedding their blood" (1992, p. 194). Skeptics are fond of citing 2 Kings 10:30 to support their position, but they often "overlook" verses 29 and 31, which state: "Jehu did not turn away from the sins of Jeroboam the son of Nebat, who had made Israel sin, that is, from the golden calves that were at Bethel and Dan.... Jehu took no heed to walk in the law of the Lord God of Israel with all his heart; for he did not depart from the sins of Jeroboam, who had made Israel sin." Jehu obeyed God's command to "strike down the house of Ahab" and utterly exterminate his descendants (2 Kings 9:

7-8; 10:30), but he did not obey God in all that he did. The passage in 2 Kings 10:29-31 indicates that even though Jehu had done what God commanded, "he did so out of a carnal zeal that was tainted with protective self-interest" (Archer, 1982, p. 208). It seems obvious that since Jehu followed in the footsteps of Israel's first wicked king by worshipping false gods and not walking according to God's law, he did not destroy Ahab's descendants out of any devotion to the Lord. Furthermore, in commentating on Jehu's actions, biblical scholar Gleason Archer noted:

> The important principle set forth in Hosea 1:4 was that when blood is shed, even in the service of God and in obedience to His command, blood-guiltiness attaches to God's agent himself if his motive was tainted with carnal self-interest rather than by a sincere concern for the purity of the faith and the preservation of God's truth (such as, for example, animated Elijah when he had the 450 prophets of Baal put to death after the contest with them on Mount Carmel) [1982, p. 209, parenthetical item in orig.].

Considering Jehu's actions by examining the motives behind those actions, solves the alleged contradiction. Jehu's failure to obey God's commands, and depart from the sins of Jeroboam, reveals that he would have equally disobeyed the other commands as well, had it been contrary to his own desires. The story of Jehu's conquest teaches a great lesson, which Albert Barnes acknowledged in his commentary on Hosea: "[I]f we do what is the will of God for any end of our own, for anything except God, we do, in fact, our own will, not God's" (1997). Indeed, just as the apostle Paul taught in his discourse on love—motives matter (1 Corinthians 13:1-3)!

DID JESUS AND THE CENTURION SPEAK TOGETHER PERSONALLY?
Matthew 8:5-13; Luke 7:1-10

On one occasion when Jesus entered Capernaum, He was asked to heal a certain centurion's servant. Skeptics allege that a contradiction exists between Matthew's account of this story (8:5-13) and Luke's account (7:1-10). Whereas Matthew's account says, "a centurion came to Him, pleading with Him" on behalf of his servant, Luke recorded that "he [the centurion—EL] sent elders of the Jews to Him, pleading with Him to come and heal his servant." Since Matthew seems to indicate that the centurion personally came to talk to Jesus, and Luke's account says that the centurion sent others to plead with Christ, skeptics contend that the two accounts are in no way harmonious. Rather, they (supposedly) represent an obvious contradiction and proof that the Bible is not the infallible Word of God.

Those who claim that such differences represent legitimate errors fail to realize that the Bible often gives "credit" to one in authority, even when others do the work. For example, when John wrote, "Pilate took Jesus and scourged Him" (19:1), he meant that Pilate ordered it to be done. Likewise, when the text says that Jesus made and baptized more disciples than John, it means that His disciples baptized more than John (John 4:1-2). In fact, the apostle John clarified this when he wrote, "though Jesus Himself did not baptize, but His disciples" (4: 2). Throughout the Bible, people are sent to speak on behalf of a person, and sometimes the text indicates that the person in position of authority actually spoke for himself, when, in fact, that person was not even present. The liaison who spoke was doing so with his authority. Today, as in times past, courts of law hold that "what a man does through a duly constituted agency, he himself actually and legally does" (Coffman, 1974, p. 105). When the president sends staff members to speak around the world on his behalf, he is the one responsible for the decisions rendered in his absence. In the same way, the centurion sent others to talk to Jesus on behalf of one of his servants. Matthew simply used a common form of speech where one attributes a certain act to a person, which is done not by himself, but by his authority (see Boles, 1952, p. 188).

One also must admit that it is possible Matthew and Luke wrote about two different accounts. Although I tend to believe that they were writing about the same incident, it is possible that Jesus had a very similar situation arise in the same town with another centurion, or the same centurion with another servant. Remember, John stated "there are also many other things that Jesus did, which if they were written one by one, I suppose that even the world itself could not contain the books that would be written" (John 21:25).

Matthew 8:5-13 and Luke 7:1-10 are in no way contradictory. By understanding that Luke simply was more specific than Matthew, and that Matthew employed a common form of speech (which we still use today), it is clear that the two accounts are harmonious.

TAKE IT, OR LEAVE IT?

Matthew 10:9-10; Mark 6:8-9; Luke 9:3

Perhaps the most difficult alleged Bible contradiction that I was asked to "tackle" in this book was presented to me some time ago by the mother of a dear friend. She asked, "When Jesus sent out the twelve apostles on what is commonly called the 'limited commission,' did He instruct them to take staffs or not?" Her question was the result of studying the three following parallel passages in the synoptic gospels (the difficult portions are in bold type).

> **"Provide neither** gold nor silver nor copper in your money belts, nor bag for your journey, nor two tunics, nor sandals, **nor staffs** (literally, "a staff"); for a worker is worthy of his food" (Matthew 10:9-10).

"He commanded them to **take nothing** for the journey **except a staff**—no bag, no bread, no copper in their money belts—but to wear sandals, and not to put on two tunics" (Mark 6:8-9).

"And He said to them, '**Take nothing** for the journey, **neither staffs** (literally, "**a staff**") nor bag nor bread nor money; and do not have two tunics apiece' " (Luke 9:3).

A cursory reading of the above passages admittedly is somewhat confusing. Matthew and Luke seem to agree that Jesus prohibited the disciples from taking a staff on their journeys, while Mark appears to give them permission to take one. Furthermore, although Luke does not record Jesus' command regarding sandals, some have concluded that Matthew and Mark also contradict each other on this point. To use the words of Steve Wells, author of *The Skeptic's Annotated Bible*, "In Matthew's gospel, Jesus tells his disciples to **go barefoot** and **take no staff**. But the Jesus in Mark's gospel (6:8-9) tells them to **wear sandals** and **carry a staff**" (emp. added). Actually then, the question at hand is about staffs and sandals, even though Luke mentioned only staffs.

The differences between Matthew and Mark are explained easily when one acknowledges that the writers used different Greek verbs to express different meanings. In Matthew, the word "provide" (NKJV) is an English translation of the Greek word *ktesthe*. According to the well-respected Greek-English lexicon by Arndt, Gingrich, and Danker, the root word comes from *ktaomai*, which means to "procure for oneself, acquire, get" (1979, p. 455). Based upon these definitions, the New American Standard Version used the English verb "acquire" in Matthew 10:9 ("Do not acquire...."), instead of "provide" or "take." In Matthew, Jesus is saying: "Do not acquire anything in addition to what you already have that may tempt you or stand in your way. Just go as you are." As Mark indicated, the apostles were to "take" (*airo*) what they had, and go. The apostles were not to waste precious time gathering supplies (extra apparel, staffs, shoes, etc.) or making preparations for their trip, but instead were instructed to trust in God's providence for additional needs. Jesus did not mean for the apostles to discard the staffs and sandals they already had; rather, they were not to go and acquire more.

To illustrate this point using a modern-day scenario, consider the CEO who came to his personnel director near the end of the day, and said that he needed her to fly to Los Angeles on a business trip immediately. If he told the director not to acquire anything for this urgent trip, including clothes, shoes, or make-up, she would know that he meant not to take anything extra. Obviously the CEO did not intend for the woman to take off her shoes, clothes, and the make-up she already was wearing in order to make the trip. Furthermore, if her boss came back five minutes later (to ensure that she understood his instructions clearly) and stated, "Hurry. The plane is leaving in one hour. Don't take anything with you except what you are wearing," the personnel director would conclude the same thing she did the first time—do not take anything extra. The CEO said the same thing using two different phrases. Similarly, the wording in Matthew and Mark represents two different ways of saying virtually the same thing.

Most apologists and biblical commentators discontinue their discussion of these parallel passages at this point. They explain the difference between Matthew and Mark's account of Jesus sending out the Twelve, but they omit Luke's account. In order to answer the skeptic's criticism adequately, however, Luke's account must be included in this discussion. Otherwise, one still is left with an unanswered alleged contradiction. The differences surrounding Luke and Mark's accounts are explainable, but it takes effort on the part of the reader to comprehend them. [The following facts must be read carefully in order to understand how the differences in these accounts do not point toward a contradiction.]

As is obvious from a comparison of the verses in Matthew and Luke, they are recording the same truth—that the apostles were not to spend valuable time gathering extra staffs—but they are using different words to do so.

> "**Provide** (Greek *ktaomi*) **neither** gold nor silver... **nor staffs**" (Matthew 10:9-10, emp. added).

> "**Take** (Greek *airo*) **nothing** for the journey, **neither staffs**" (Luke 9:3, emp. added).

Luke did not use *ktaomi* in his account because he nearly always used *ktaomai* in a different sense than Matthew did. In Matthew's account, the word *ktaomai* is used to mean "provide" or "acquire," whereas in the books of Luke and Acts, Luke used this word to mean "purchase, buy, or earn." Notice the following examples of how Luke used this word.

> "I fast twice a week; I pay tithes of all that I **get**" (*ktaomai*) [Luke 18:12, emp. added, NAS]

> "Now this man **purchased** (*ktaomai*) a field with the wages of iniquity (Acts 1:18, emp. added).

> "Your money perish with you, because you thought that the gift of God could be **purchased** (*ktaomai*) with money!" (Acts 8:20, emp. added).

> "The commander answered, 'With a large sum I **obtained** (*ktaomai*) this citizenship' " (Acts 22:28, emp. added).

> [Luke 21:19 is the only place where one could argue that Luke may have used *ktaomai* to mean something other than "purchase, buy, or earn." But, even in this verse a transactional notion is present (Miller, 1997)].

When Luke, the beloved physician (Colossians 4:14), used the word *ktaomai*, he meant something different than when Matthew, the tax collector, used the same word. Whereas Luke used *ktaomai* to refer to purchasing or buying something, Matthew used the Greek verb *agorazo* (cf. Matthew 14:15; 25:9-10; 27:6-7). Matthew used *ktaomai* only in the sense of acquiring something (not purchasing something). As such, it would make absolutely no sense for Luke to use ktaomai in his account of Jesus sending out the apostles (9:3). If he did, then he would have Jesus forbidding the apostles to "purchase" or "buy" money ["**Buy** nothing for the journey, neither staffs nor bag nor bread nor money...."]. Thus, Luke used the more general Greek verb (*airo*) in order to convey the same idea that Matthew did when using the Greek verb *ktaomai*.

Just as *ktaomai* did not mean the same for Luke and Matthew, the Greek word *airo* (translated "take" in both Mark 6:8 and Luke 9:3) often did not mean the same for Luke and Mark (see Miller, 1997). [Understanding this simple fact eliminates the "contradiction" completely, for unless the skeptic can be certain that Mark and Luke were using the word in the same sense, he cannot prove that the accounts contradict each other.] Mark consistently used *airo* in other passages throughout his gospel to mean simply "take" or "pick up and carry" (2:9; 6:29; 11:23; 13:16). That Luke (in 9:3) did not mean the same sense of *airo* as Mark did (in 6:8) is suggested by the fact that in Luke 19:21-22, he used this same verb to mean "acquire." Another piece of comparative data between Mark and Luke is that when Mark recorded Jesus informing His listeners that to be His disciple, one had to "take up his cross" (Mark 8:34), he used the word *airo*. Luke, on the other hand, used the Greek word *bastazo* (14:27) [Miller, 1997].

Without going any farther with these language comparisons, one simply must understand that the Greek language (like most languages) is flexible enough so that sometimes two writers can use the same word to mean different things, and sometimes they can use different words to mean the same thing (as indicated by the following chart,* which serves as a summary of the comparisons and contrasts made above).

	ktaomai	*agorazo*	*airo*	*bastazo*
Matthew	to acquire	to purchase, buy		
Mark			to take, pick up and carry	
Luke	to purchase, buy		to acquire	to take, pick up and carry

*NOTE: Only the definitions that pertain to the particular verses in question are shown.

In case you think such "language leeway" in the Greek sounds absurd, remember that this flexibility appears frequently in the English language. Consider two basketball coaches who are commenting on a player. One says, "He is bad;" the other says, "He is good." The coaches may be using two different words to mean the same thing. The truth is, in some contexts the words "bad" and "good" are opposites, in other situations they are synonymous.

Although many have been misled about the differences regarding Jesus' instructions when sending out His apostles on the limited commission, the truth is that Matthew, Mark, and Luke were all saying the same thing: "Hurry up and get moving!"

WAS THE ROBE PLACED ON
JESUS SCARLET OR PURPLE?

Matthew 27:27-28; Mark 15:16-17; John 19:1-2

After being flogged with a dreadful Roman scourge, Jesus was taken by Pilate's soldiers into the governor's headquarters where the whole garrison gathered around Him. It was here that the soldiers placed a crown of thorns on His head, a reed in His hand, and a robe on His body. But what color was the robe that was placed on Jesus' marred body? Whereas Matthew said that the soldiers "put **a scarlet robe**" on Jesus (27:27-28), Mark noted that "they clothed Him with **purple**" (15:16-17), and John stated that the soldiers put **"a purple robe"** on Him (19:1-2). Does a valid answer exist for the differences in the gospel narratives concerning the robe placed upon Jesus after His scourging?

All would agree that we oftentimes see colors a little differently. What one person calls blue, someone else may (in a more specific fashion) call navy blue. A die-hard football fan may refer to his team's color as dark red, whereas someone else who sees the team's faded uniforms for the first time at the end of a grueling season may conclude that the team's color is more maroon. While coloring pictures for their parents, one child may color a yellow-orange Sun, while the other draws a Sun that is bright yellow. Surely no one would accuse these individuals of lying or being deceitful because one was more specific than another. Likewise, skeptics have no solid ground on which to stand when they disregard common sense and create biblical contradictions that do not exist. The simple fact is, Matthew, Mark, Luke, and John wrote from different perspectives; they did not participate in collusion. The same way that individuals today look at colors and see different tones, shades, and tints, the gospel writers saw the activities surrounding the life of Jesus from different angles.

The garment placed upon Jesus after His brutal scourging likely was similar to faded football uniforms, but in His case we read of "a scarlet robe...faded to resemble purple" (*Wycliffe Bible Commentary*, 1985). [It is difficult to imagine Pilate arraying Jesus' bloody body with a new robe. More likely it was one that had been worn and cast off as worthless.] Furthermore, according to A.T. Robertson, there were various shades of purple and scarlet in the first century, and it was not easy to distinguish the colors or tints (1997). In fact, the ancients (and especially the Romans) used the term purple when speaking of various shades of red. Consequently, these different colors sometimes would be called by the same name.

As one can see, there is no discrepancy in the gospel narratives concerning the color of the robe Jesus wore. Just like others of their day, the gospel writers simply used the terms scarlet and purple interchangeably.

DEAD, OR DYING?
Matthew 19:18; Mark 5:23; Luke 8:42

After healing the men who were possessed with demons on the east shore of the Sea of Galilee (Matthew 8:28-34), Jesus passed over to the other side and "came into his own city." Soon thereafter a man by the name of Jairus, one of the rulers of the synagogue, fell at Jesus' feet and worshipped Him, saying, "My daughter has just died, but come and lay Your hand on her and she will live" (Matthew 9:18). Normally, we would continue telling this wonderful story and rehearse how Jesus raised the twelve-year-old girl from the dead. However, the purpose here is to answer the skeptics who claim that a contradiction exists between Matthew's account of this story and the accounts recorded by Mark and Luke. Whereas Matthew records Jairus telling Jesus, "My daughter **has just died**" (Matthew 19:18, emp. added), the other two accounts indicate that his daughter was "**at the point of death**" (Mark 5:23, emp. added) and that "**she was dying**" (Luke 8:42, emp. added).

Critics of the Bible's inerrancy assert that the difference in these accounts represents a blatant contradiction.

Various Greek scholars and commentators have stated that there is not as much difference between Matthew's *arti eteleutesn* ("has just died;" cf. Hebrews 11:22) and *eschates echer* ("is dying" NIV) in Mark 5:23 as some would have us to think. According to Craig Blomberg, *arti* ("even now" or "just") has some connotations that suggest not always a **present** reality, but an **inevitable** reality (cf. Matthew 3:15; 23:39; 1 Corinthians 4:13). Therefore, Blomberg concluded that it is possible Matthew was relating the inevitability and certainty of Jairus' daughter dying, rather than making a statement about her current condition (1992, p. 160). Adam Clarke mentioned in his commentary on Matthew that 9:18 could be translated, "my daughter was just now dying" (1996). Albert Barnes agreed, saying: "The Greek word, rendered 'is even now dead,' does not of necessity mean, as our translation would express, that she had actually expired, but only that she was 'dying' or about to die.... The passage [Matthew 9:18–EL] may be expressed thus: 'My daughter was so sick that she must be by this time dead'" (1997). In short, the alleged contradiction may be a simple misunderstanding of what Matthew actually wrote about the dying child.

A better explanation to this alleged discrepancy is that Jairus uttered both statements: Mark and Luke mention her severe sickness, while Matthew speaks of her death. As in so many other places, each writer reported only a part of what occurred and what was said. Does Matthew's omission of the coming of the messengers who told Jairus that his daughter had just died mean that his account contradicts the others (Mark 5:35; Luke 8:49)? Certainly not! Nor do his additional details. R.C. Trench, in his classic work on the miracles of Jesus, made the following observation concerning the differences in the gospel writers' accounts of what was said when Jairus approached Jesus:

> When the father left the child, she was at her last gasp; and he knew not whether to regard her now as dead or alive; and, yet having not received certain knowledge of her death, he was perplexed whether to speak of her as departed or not, **expressing himself one moment in one language, and at the next in another.** Strange that a circumstance like this, so drawn from life, so testifying of the things recorded, should be urged by some as a contradiction (1949, pp. 107-108, emp. added).

Strange Indeed!

HOW DID JUDAS KILL HIMSELF?
Matthew 27:5; Acts 1:18

Through the years, the description of Judas Iscariot's death has been one of the most popular alleged Bible contradictions. Whereas Matthew records that Judas "went and hanged himself" after betraying Jesus for 30 pieces of silver (27:5), Luke records that "falling headlong, he burst open in the middle and all his entrails gushed out" (Acts 1:18). Because Matthew mentions only a hanging, and Luke mentions Judas falling headfirst and bursting open at his midsection, a "real" contradiction supposedly is staring us in the face.

The truth of the matter is, like the accounts of Jesus' resurrection, these two verses simply supplement each other; it is not an either/or scenario. Rather, Judas "hanged himself," and sometime later fell headfirst, causing his midsection open to burst open.

Consider the following: Many types of bacteria live inside the body. Bacteria generally are the first to begin the process of decomposition after an organism dies. Saprobic bacteria invade every inch of the dead body, and begin decomposing and digesting the organic tissue. As they decompose organic material to produce energy, these microorganisms help recycle nutrients such as nitrogen and carbon back into the environment. In accomplishing this, the bacteria produce significant quantities of gaseous by-products. Now, if Judas' body had been dead for several days, the gases present would begin to exert considerable pressure on the abdomen, causing his midsection to burst open easily upon hitting the hard ground.

Matthew 27:5 and Acts 1:18 cannot be accepted as legitimately contradicting each other if it is possible for both to be true—and it certainly is possible for both incidents to have occurred. Consider a brawl in which two men are fighting to the death. The larger man strikes the undersized man in the throat, crushing his larynx. For nearly 60 seconds, the wounded man stumbles around trying to breathe, but to no avail. He then goes limp, falls to the ground, and strikes his head on the cement, having died from asphyxia. When the police come to the scene and ask witnesses what happened, one person will likely declare, "James struck John and killed him." Another person may say, "John suffocated," while another might add, "Falling headfirst, John busted his skull on the ground, causing part of his brain to ooze out onto the concrete." Are the witnesses' statements contradictory? No. They are supplementary. Likewise, neither of the statements concerning the death of Judas is contradictory; one does not exclude the other.

According to ancient tradition, Judas hanged himself above the Valley of Hinnom on the edge of a cliff. Eventually the rope snapped (or was cut or untied), thus causing Judas to fall headfirst into the field below, as Luke described. Matthew does not deny that Judas fell and had his entrails gush out, and Luke does not deny that Judas hanged himself. In short, Matthew records the **method** in which Judas attempted his death. Luke reports the end **result**.

WHO BOUGHT THE POTTER'S FIELD?
Matthew 27:5-6; Acts 1:18

The description of Judas' death is not the only problem skeptics have with Acts 1:18. Since Matthew 27:5-6 says the **chief priests** used the betrayal money that Judas threw on the temple floor to purchase the potter's field, critics contend that a contradiction exists because Acts 1:18 indicates that **Judas** purchased the field with the blood money. Obviously, Judas could not have purchased the field because he gave the 30 pieces of silver back to the priests before hanging himself. Thus, to say that Judas bought the potter's field is incorrect...right? Wrong!

I suppose that if common sense and unbiased reasoning were omitted from this discussion, then one might conclude that these differences represent a legitimate contradiction. If one believes it is wrong to say a father bought a car for his son, when in actuality the son purchased the car with $5,000 his father gave him, then I suppose that Acts 1:18 and Matthew 27:5-6 are contradictory. If one believes that it is wrong to say an employer purchased a meal for his staff, when it really was one of the employees who handed the money to the waiter, then the events recorded in Acts 1:18 could be considered fictitious. But what reasonable person would reach such conclusions as these?

Acts 1:18 simply informs us that Judas furnished the means of purchasing the field. One is not forced to conclude that Judas **personally** bought the potter's field. As in modern-day writings and speeches, it is very common for the Scriptures to represent a man as doing a thing when, in fact, he merely supplies the means for doing it. For example, Joseph spoke of his brothers as selling him into Egypt (Genesis 45:4-5; cf. Acts 7:9), when actually they sold him to the Ishmaelites (who then sold him into Egypt). And, as mentioned earlier in this chapter, John wrote that "the Pharisees had heard that Jesus made and baptized more disciples than John (**though Jesus Himself did not baptize, but His disciples**)" (John 4:1-3, emp. added). The same principle is recognized in law in the well-known Latin maxim, "*Qui facit per alium, facit per se*," which means "he who acts through another is deemed in law to do it himself."

Whether one says that Judas "purchased a field with the wages of iniquity" (Acts 1:18), or that the chief priests "bought with them the potter's field" (Matthew 27:7), he has stated the same truth, only in different ways.

HAS MAN SEEN GOD?
John 1:18; Exodus 33:20; Genesis 32:30

In John 1:18, the apostle wrote: "No one has seen God at any time." In Exodus 33:20 God said to Moses: "You cannot see My face; for no man can see Me and live." But Genesis 32:30 records Jacob as saying: "For I have seen God face to face, and my life is preserved." Have John and Moses—certainly two of the most influential writers in the Bible—contradicted each other as infidels and skeptics have suggested?

No, they have not. The "contradiction" is the result of the passages being taken out of the context in which they were written originally. Although these passages may **seem** to contradict each other, when considered in their appropriate context, they do not because they are not speaking of God being "seen" in the same sense. Several illustrations of this principle can be found in Scripture.

First, consider Moses "seeing" God in a burning bush (Exodus 3:2ff.). He saw a fire on the side of a mountain. When he went to investigate, he saw a bush that burned but was not consumed. As he observed this unusual sight, God called to him from the midst of the bush and said, "Moses, Moses!" And Moses said, "Here I am." Then the voice from the burning bush echoed: "I am the God of your father—the God of Abraham, the God of Isaac, and the God of Jacob" (Exodus 3:6a). The text indicates that "Moses hid his face, for **he was afraid to look upon God**" (3:6b, emp. added).

As Moses spoke to the burning bush on the mountainside, was he addressing God? Indeed he was, as the passage clearly teaches. But does the passage also teach that as he looked at the bush, Moses was fearful because he considered it "seeing"

God? Yes, Exodus 3:6 so states. But, when Moses looked upon the burning bush, did he **actually** "see" God? No. He saw an image that we as humans can comprehend. The bush was a **representation** of God–an occasion where something took God's place.

Second, consider Job's "seeing" God in a whirlwind (Job 38:1ff.). Job made a wrongful boast that landed him in serious trouble with God. Suddenly (and unexpectedly), a whirlwind appeared before Job–from which the voice of God echoed: "Who is this who darkens counsel by words without knowledge? Now prepare yourself like a man; I will question you, and you shall answer me" (Job 38:2-3). Job looked at the whirlwind and heard God. But was God really **in** the whirlwind? Did Job actually **see** God when he looked into this magnificent force of nature? No. Instead, Job saw a **manifestation** of God that a human could comprehend. The whirlwind "took God's place."

Third, consider Jacob's "seeing" God as he wrestled with an angel (Genesis 32:24-30). He wrestled from night until daybreak with this heavenly being and eventually said: "**I have seen God face to face**." Was it really God that Jacob saw? No, he did not see God, but instead witnessed a representative of God. A similar example can be found in the case of Manoah (the father of Samson), recorded in Judges 13. In this instance, the text says that Manoah and his wife were visited by the "Angel of the Lord" (13:13) who informed them of their son's impending birth. Afterwards, Manoah said: "We shall surely die because **we have seen God!**" (13:22). Again, it is necessary to ask: Was it really God that Manoah and his wife saw? No, they did not see God but instead witnessed (just as Jacob had) a manifestation of God via the angel. [NOTE: A fascinating parallel can be seen in Gideon's statement in Judges 6:22 when he cried: "I have seen the Angel of the Lord **face to face**."]

What, then, is the explanation of the alleged contradiction between passages such as John 1:18, Exodus 33:20, and Genesis 32:30? How can the Scriptures state that "no man hath seen God" (John 1:18) or that "no man shall see Me and live" (Exodus 33:20), while stating elsewhere that Jacob saw God "face to face" (Genesis 32:30) and that Manoah and his wife had "seen God" (Judges 6:22)? E.G. Sewell and David Lipscomb provided a partial answer to this kind of question when they wrote: "When Jacob is represented as saying he saw God, it was only an angel of God that appeared to him in the form of a man. In Hosea it is called an **angel** so that in that case Jacob did not see the face of God at all, but only an angel of God" (1921, p. 274, emp. in orig.).

An illustration of this very point can be found in the incarnation of Jesus. The apostle Paul, in discussing Christ's deity, noted that as a member of the Godhead, Jesus had existed throughout eternity and possessed "equality with God" (Philippians 2:5-6). He also discussed the fact, however, that Christ –Who had existed in heaven "in the form of God"–took on the "likeness of men" (1:7) while He was on Earth. Was Christ equal to God? Yes, He was. Did men **see** Christ during His earthly ministry? Yes, they did. Did they therefore "see" God? Yes, indeed. But did they see God's true image (i.e., as a spirit Being–John 4:24), or did they see instead an **embodiment** of God as Jesus dwelt here in a fleshly form? The answer is obvious from John's explanation in the first few verses of the first chapter of his gospel. All this makes it clear that while Jesus is God, He also became a man "so that in history he might reveal the God whom no man has ever seen" (Pack, 1975, p. 39).

Has man seen God? Yes and no. Although he has seen manifestations of God, man has never "seen" Him in His true image (as a spirit Being).

DID YOU HEAR THAT?

Acts 9:7; 22:9

In the account of the Lord's appearance to Saul on the road to Damascus–recorded by Luke in Acts 9, and then related in Paul's address in Acts 22–there **appears** to be a contradiction. Acts 9:7 records that the men traveling with Saul (known later as the apostle Paul) **heard** a voice; while Paul states in Acts 22:9 that they **did not hear** a voice. Is there a contradiction here?

Admittedly, at first glance the two passages under consideration do **seem** to be in direct opposition. Apologists have acknowledged this difficulty for many years, and have offered at least two plausible explanations. First, it could be that Acts 22:9 has been mistranslated. Instead of being translated, "And those who were with me indeed saw the light and were afraid, but they **did not hear** the voice of Him who spoke to me," the latter part of the verse actually should read: "but they **did not understand** the voice of Him who spoke to me." If this translation were correct, it would put to rest any suggestion of contradiction.

Believer-turned-infidel Dan Barker, however, has refused steadfastly to accept such a solution, and has argued that the Greek word for "hear" (*akouo*) does not mean "understand" (except in a few special situations such as 1 Corinthians 14:2). There are other passages, he has noted, where *akouo* does mean "understand," but in each case it is linked explicitly with the word "understand." As an example, he has cited Matthew 13:13, which reads: "Therefore speak I to them in parables; because seeing they see not, and hearing [*akouo*] they hear [*akouo*] not, neither do they understand" (ASV). Mr. Barker believes that if the second *akouo* meant "understand," then it would not have been necessary for Luke to include the last phrase, "neither do they understand." According to the article on his Web site dealing with this matter, "this underscores the fact that gram-

mar is not enough to determine when *akouo* might be translated loosely" (Barker, 1994). I would like to note, though, that
had Matthew omitted the last phrase, we still would have understood the second "hear" to mean "understand." Otherwise,
Jesus would have been saying, "They hear my words, but they
do not hear my words." In similar fashion, we can understand
Acts 22:9 to mean, "the men perceived a voice, but they did
not understand the words spoken."

Whereas it may be that the word "understand" should be
used instead of "hear" in Acts 22:9, others are of the opinion
it is Acts 9:7 that has not been translated as accurately as possible. According to them, the verse should read: "And the men
that journeyed with him stood speechless, hearing **the sound**
[as opposed to "the voice"] but beholding no man." Various
highly respected Greek scholars have proposed this very argument as a solution to the alleged discrepancy. In fact, the
man known affectionately among theologians as the "dean
of Greek scholars," A.T. Robertson, wrote in regard to the difference in cases:

> In 22:9 Paul says that the men "beheld the light" (*to
> men phos etheasanto*), but evidently did not discern the
> person. Paul also says there, "but they heard not the
> voice of him that spake to me" (*ten de phonen ouk ekousan
> tou lalountos moi*). Instead of this being a flat contra-
> diction of what Luke says in 9:7 it is natural to take it
> as being likewise (as with the "light" and "no one") a
> distinction between the "sound" (original sense of *phone*
> as in John 3:8) and the separate words spoken. It so
> happens that *akouo* is used either with the accusative
> (the extent of the hearing) or the genitive (the speci-
> fying). It is possible that such a distinction here coin-
> cides with the two senses of *phone*. They heard a sound
> (9:7), but did not understand the words (22:9) [1930,
> 3:117-118, parenthetical items in orig.].

Consider also the words of Greek expert Ray Summers:

> Some verbs take their object in a case other than the accusative. There is a variety of usage at this point. *Akouo* may take its object in the genitive or the accusative. Usually *akouo* with the genitive means "to hear without understanding." This probably explains the difficulty involved in Acts 9:7 and 22:9. The incident is the experience of Paul in seeing the light and hearing the voice on the road to Damascus. Acts 9:7 states that Paul's companions heard the voice (*akouo* with the genitive); Acts 22:9 says they did not hear the voice (*akouo* with the accusative). Thus both constructions say the same thing; the companions of Paul did not understand what the voice said to Paul; to them it was unintelligible sound. (1950, p. 51)

Numerous other Greek scholars have expressed the same viewpoint (see, for example: Arndt and Gingrich, 1957, pp. 31-33; Thayer; 1979, pp. 22-23; Vincent, 1975, p. 571; and Vine, 1985, p. 296). The word "hear" in Acts 22:9 **can** be used to indicate that it was a sound—not a voice—that the men heard on the road to Damascus.

Interestingly, we have been given a parallel to the event recorded in Acts 9—John 12:28-29. Here, just as in the passage in Acts, we have Jehovah speaking from heaven to a man (Jesus, in this instance). After the Lord spoke, notice the people's response as recorded in verse 29: "Therefore the people who stood by and heard it said that it had thundered. Others said, 'An angel has spoken to Him.' " So amazing and frightening was the sound of God's voice that the multitude was not quite sure what to make of it. The voice must have reverberated like thunder, yet it was discernible enough that some mistakenly thought it was the voice of an angel. Had the crowd been interviewed, some would have said, "We heard no voice, only thunder," while others would have responded differently by saying, "Well, it sounded to us like a voice, maybe the voice of an angel." Both groups of people undoubtedly **heard something** when God spoke, but not everyone present **understood** what was said. The same could be true of the men who traveled with Saul on the way to Damascus—they heard something, but not everyone present understood what was said.

JAMES' "MISSING QUOTE"
James 4:5

In addressing the passage found in James 4:5, Albert Barnes wrote: "Few passages of the New Testament have given expositors more perplexity than this" (1972, p. 70). When one reads this verse from some versions of the Bible, it seems that the writer referred to a quotation from the Old Testament that actually does not exist. Skeptics sometimes use this verse in attempts to "prove" that Bible writers often were mistaken, and therefore not inspired by a higher Being. Can this "perplexity" be explained logically? It most certainly can.

In context, the passage reads as follows (the highlighted section is the particular portion in question):

> Ye adulterers and adulteresses, know ye not that the friendship of the world is enmity with God? Whosoever therefore will be a friend of the world is the enemy of God. **Do ye think that the scripture saith in vain, The spirit that dwelleth in us lusteth to envy?** But he giveth more grace. Wherefore he saith, God resisteth the proud, but giveth grace unto the humble. Submit yourselves therefore to God. Resist the devil, and he will flee from you (James 4:4-7, KJV).

> Unfaithful creatures! Do you not know that friendship with the world is enmity with God? Therefore, whoever wishes to be a friend of the world makes himself an enemy of God. **Or do you suppose it is in vain that the scripture says, "He yearns jealously over the spirit which he has made to dwell in**

us"? But he gives more grace; therefore it says, "God opposes the proud, but gives grace to the humble." Submit yourselves therefore to God. Resist the devil and he will flee from you (James 4:4-7, RSV).

The KJV and RSV separate verse five into two sections. The first introduces a supposed quote with the phrase "the scripture says," and draws attention to the second section, which seems to highlight the quotation either via quotation marks (as in the RSV) or by capitalizing the first word of the quote (as in the KJV). According to those attempting to discredit the Bible, this verse "proves" that the Bible is false since the supposed quotation is found nowhere in Scripture.

With some careful study, one finds that the controversy can be explained fairly simply. When James' comment is considered in its context, and is translated correctly, it becomes apparent that he did not intend for the second half of the verse to be taken as a **direct quotation** from the Old Testament. The translations provided by the King James Version, Revised Standard Version, and others that render the verse as a quotation, are incorrect. [It is important to realize that the manuscripts with which translators work contain little or no punctuation. Thus, the translators must exercise some discretion when implementing punctuation marks in the text.]

Such a suggestion raises the question as to what the correct translation is for the passage. Several solutions have been presented, the most likely of which being that James did not intend to quote a **specific verse**, but instead was referring to **ideas and concepts** found throughout the whole of the Old Testament. In his commentary on the books of Hebrews and James, R.C.H. Lenski wrote:

> Many pages have been written regarding the different interpretations of v. 5 and the discussions of these interpretations. We confine ourselves to two points. We are not convinced that the question is a formula

of quotation. Such a formula has never been used: "Do you think that the Scripture speaks in an empty way?" If a quotation **were** to follow, we should certainly expect the addition "saying that."

What follows has never been verified as being a quotation; nothing like it has been found in any writing as all admit. The fact that the Scripture does not speak in an empty way refers to v. 4 which presents as a teaching of Scripture the truth that friendship of the world is enmity against God, etc. The idea is not that this is a quotation, but that it is a teaching of Scripture and by no means empty (1966, p. 631, emp. in orig.).

The late Bible scholar, Guy N. Woods, supported the idea of James' reference being, not to a specific quote, but rather to a general concept within the Old Testament writings. He cited Genesis 6:3-7, Exodus 29:5, Deuteronomy 32:1-21, Job 5:12, Ecclesiastes 4:4, and Proverbs 27:4 as verses where the thought behind James 4:5 is conveyed (1972, p. 214). Several commentators believe that James' statement represents a "condensation" of the Old Testament rather than an exact quotation—a position that fits the context of the verse, and solves the problem of the "missing quote."

The late, respected Greek scholar J.W. Roberts was correct in saying that the 1901 American Standard Version provides the closest match to the true meaning (1977, p. 129).

Ye adulteresses, know ye not that the friendship of the world is enmity with God? Whosoever therefore would be a friend of the world maketh himself an enemy of God. **Or think ye that the scripture speaketh in vain? Doth the spirit which he made to dwell in us long unto envying?** But he giveth more grace. Wherefore the scripture saith, God resisteth the proud, but giveth grace to the humble. Be subject therefore

unto God; but resist the devil, and he will flee from
you (James 4:4-7, ASV, emp. added).

Hugo McCord, in his independent translation of the New
Testament, rendered James 4:5 very much like the American
Standard Version, with a slight updating of language. His trans-
lation reads: "Do you think that the scripture speaks emptily?
Does the Spirit living in us lust to envy?" (1988, p. 442).

Regardless of which version is used, it appears that James
did not intend this verse to be taken as a quotation. The most
likely answer is that James did indeed refer to ideas and thoughts
expressed throughout the entire Old Testament, rather than
quoting a specific verse.

AFTERWORD

Skeptics who attack God's Word with unsupported allegations will continue to fail. The Bible is and always has been the inerrant Word of God (2 Timothy 3:16-17; 2 Peter 1:20-21). Based upon the evidence we have, **it is reasonable** to believe that Bible is inspired by God. There is no other book like it on the planet. Evidence to substantiate the Bible's claims of its own inspiration can be drawn from such external evidence as the historical documentation of biblical people, places, and events, or archaeological artifacts that corroborate biblical statements or circumstances. The internal evidence includes the Bible's unity, predictive prophecy, and scientific foreknowledge (to list just three examples). The Bible is unparalleled in human history and bears testimony to the fact that the very existence of it cannot be explained in any other way except to acknowledge that it is the result of an overriding, superintending, guiding Mind.

The belief that the Bible is the inerrant Word of God is not based upon wishful thinking, but upon the reasonable examination of facts. As this book has shown, when a person takes a little time and effort to analyze the allegations skeptics have made (and continue to make) concerning the Bible, the truth becomes evident: The Bible is innocent of the charges levied against it. It has been tried, and shown to be true. Like the black-smith's anvil—which wears out many hammers but itself re-mains unaffected—over time the Bible wears out the skeptics' innocuous charges, all the while remaining unscathed. Truly, it is the inerrant Word of God.

In volume two of *The Anvil Rings*, I plan to discuss many more alleged Bible discrepancies. The book will present dis-cussions and answer questions regarding God's attributes, the teachings, actions, and Deity of Christ, the Noahic Flood, and the differences in various "salvation passages." It will answer a variety of questions regarding alleged ethical contradictions, the accuracy of the Bible when compared to science and his-tory, and it will address allegations concerning biblical chro-nology, the Christian's conduct, and differences between the Old and New Testaments. Plus, there will be a lengthy discus-sion on evidences proving the Bible's inspiration.

The principles discussed in this two-volume set should help the Bible reader to not only answer the skeptics' objections, but also to resolve apparent contradictions he or she might encounter in daily Bible study. With both volumes in hand, a person should be able to know (without a doubt) that the Bi-ble is error-free and God-given.

REFERENCES

Albright, W.F. (1938), "Archaeology Confronts Biblical Criticism," *The American Scholar*, 7:186, April.

The American Heritage Dictionary of the English Language (2000), (Boston, MA: Houghton Mifflin), fourth edition.

"Animal Kingdom" (1988), *The New Unger's Bible Dictionary* (Electronic Database: Biblesoft), originally published by Moody Press, Chicago, Illinois.

Archer, Gleason L. (1964), *A Survey of Old Testament Introduction* (Chicago, IL: Moody).

Archer, Gleason L. (1970), "Old Testament History and Recent Archaeology from Abraham to Moses," *Bibliotheca Sacra*, 127:3-25, January.

Archer, Gleason L. (1982), *An Encyclopedia of Bible Difficulties* (Grand Rapids, MI: Zondervan).

Arndt, William (1955), *Does the Bible Contradict Itself?* (St. Louis, MO: Concordia).

Arndt, William and F.W. Gingrich (1957), *A Greek-English Lexicon of the New Testament and other Early Christian Literature* (Chicago, IL: University of Chicago Press).

Arndt, William and F.W. Gingrich (1967), *A Greek-English Lexicon of the New Testament and Other Early Christian Literature* (Chicago, IL: University of Chicago Press).

Arndt, William, F.W. Gingrich, and Frederick Danker (1979), *A Greek-English Lexicon of the New Testament and Other Early Christian Literature* (Chicago, IL: University of Chicago Press).

Barclay, William (1959), *The Letters to the Philippians, Colossians and Thessalonians* (Philadelphia, PA: Westminster).

Barker, Dan (1992), *Losing Faith in Faith* (Madison, WI: Freedom From Religion Foundation, Inc.).

Barker, Dan (1994), [On-line], URL: http://www.infidels.org/library/magazines/tsr/1994/1/1voice94.html.

Barnes, Albert (1949), *Notes on the Old and New Testaments: Acts* (Grand Rapids, MI: Baker).

Barnes, Albert (1972 reprint), *Notes on the Old and New Testaments: James, Peter, John, and Jude* (Grand Rapids, MI: Baker).

Barnes, Albert (1997), *Notes on the Old and New Testaments* (Electronic Database: Biblesoft).

Blomberg, Craig L. (1992), *Matthew* (Nashville, TN: Broadman).

Boles, H. Leo (1940), *A Commentary on the Gospel According to Luke* (Nashville, TN: Gospel Advocate).

Boles, H. Leo (1952), *A Commentary on the Gospel According to Matthew* (Nashville, TN: Gospel Advocate).

Brown, Andrew (1999), *The Darwin Wars* (New York: Simon and Schuster).

Bruce, F.F. (1953), *The New Testament Documents—Are They Reliable?* (Grand Rapids, MI: Eerdmans), fourth edition.

Bruce, F.F. (1988), *The Book of Acts* (Grand Rapids, MI: Eerdmans), revised edition.

Burrows, Millar (1941), *What Mean These Stones?* (New Haven, CT: American Schools of Oriental Research).

Cansdale, George (1970), *All the Animals of the Bible Lands* (Grand Rapids, MI: Zondervan).

Cansdale, George (1996), "Animals of the Bible," *New Bible Dictionary*, ed. J.D. Douglas (Downers Grove, IL: InterVarsity Press), third edition.

Cassuto, U. (1961), *A Commentary on the Book of Genesis* (Jerusalem: Magnes).

Cheyne, T.K., ed. (1899), *Encyclopedia Biblica* (London: A & C Black).

Clarke, Adam (no date), *Clarke's Commentary on the Old Testament–Volume I: Genesis to Deuteronomy* (New York: Abingdon-Cokesbury).

Clarke, Adam (1996), *Adam Clarke's Commentary* (Electronic Database: Biblesoft).

Clayton, Peter A. (2001), *Chronicle of the Pharaohs* (London: Thames & Hudson).

Clements, Tad S. (1990), *Science vs. Religion* (Buffalo, NY: Prometheus).

"Cock" (1998), *Fausset's Bible Dictionary* (Electronic Database: Biblesoft).

"Cock-crowing," McClintock, John and James Strong (1968), *Cyclopaedia of Biblical Theological and Ecclesiastical Literature* (Grand Rapids, MI: Baker).

Coffman, James Burton (1971), *Commentary on the Gospel of Matthew* (Abilene, TX: ACU Press).

Coffman, James Burton (1974), *Commentary on the Gospel of Matthew* (Abilene, TX: ACU Press).

Coffman, James Burton (1985a), *Commentary on Exodus* (Abilene, TX: ACU Press).

Coffman, James Burton (1985b), *Commentary on Genesis* (Abilene, TX: ACU Press).

DeHaan, M.R. (1978), *Genesis and Evolution* (Grand Rapids, MI: Zondervan).

Dillard, Raymond B. and Tremper Longman III (1994), *An Introduction to the Old Testament* (Grand Rapids, MI: Zondervan).

Dungan, D.R. (1888), *Hermeneutics* (Delight, AR: Gospel Light), reprint.

"The Extant Writings of Julius Africanus" (1994 reprint), *Ante-Nicene Fathers* (Grand Rapids, MI: Eerdmans), pp. 125-140.

Fairbairn, P. (1957 reprint), "Genealogies," *Fairbairn's Imperial Standard Bible Encyclopedia* (Grand Rapids, MI: Zondervan), 2:351.

Fee, Gordon D. (1987), *The First Epistle to the Corinthians* (Grand Rapids: Eerdmans).

Finkelstein, Israel and Neil Asher Silberman (2001), *The Bible Unearthed* (New York: The Free Press).

Foster, R.C. (1971), *Studies in the Life of Christ* (Grand Rapids, MI: Baker).

Frank, H.T. (1964), *An Archaeological Companion to the Bible* (London: SCM Press).

Free, Joseph P. (1944), "Abraham's Camels," *Journal of Near Eastern Studies*, 3:187-193, July.

Free, Joseph P. and Howard F. Vos (1992), *Archaeology and Bible History* (Grand Rapids, MI: Zondervan).

Gaussen, L. (1949), *The Inspiration of the Holy Scriptures*, trans. David D. Scott (Chicago, IL: Moody).

Geisler, Norman L. and Ronald M. Brooks (1990), *When Skeptics Ask* (Wheaton, IL: Victor Books).

Geisler, Norman L. and Thomas A. Howe (1992), *When Critics Ask* (Wheaton, IL: Victor Books).

Geisler, Norman L. and William E. Nix (1986), *A General Introduction to the Bible* (Chicago, IL: Moody), revised edition.

"Genealogy," (1986), *Nelson's Illustrated Bible Dictionary* (Electronic Database: Biblesoft), orig. published by Thomas Nelson Publishers of Nashville, Tennessee.

Godet, Frederic (1890), *Gospel of Luke* (Edinburgh: T&T Clark).

Gottwald, Norman (1959), *A Light to the Nations* (New York: Harper and Row).

Green, William Henry (1978), *The Higher Criticism of the Pentateuch* (Grand Rapids, MI: Baker).

Greenleaf, Simon (1995), *The Testimony of the Evangelists* (Grand Rapids, MI: Kregel Classics).

Guthrie, Donald (1990), *New Testament Introduction* (Downers Grove, IL: InterVarsity Press).

Haley, John W. (1951), *Alleged Discrepancies of the Bible* (Nashville, TN: Gospel Advocate), reprint.

Hamilton, Victor P. (1990), *The Book of Genesis: Chapters 1-17* (Grand Rapids, MI: Eerdmans).

Hamilton, Victor P. (1995), *The Book of Genesis: Chapters 18-50* (Grand Rapids, MI: Eerdmans).

Harman, Henry M. (1878), *Introduction to the Holy Scriptures* (New York: Eaton and Mains).

Harrison, R.K. (1963), *The Archaeology of the Old Testament* (New York: Harper and Row).

Hasel, Gerhard F. (1980), "Genesis 5 and 11: Chronologies in the Biblical History of Beginnings," *Origins*, 7[1]:23-37, [Online], URL: http://www.ldolphin.org/haselgeneal.html.

Hendrix, Eddie (1976), "What About Those Copyist Errors?" *Firm Foundation*, 93[14]:5, April 6.

Hoehner, Harold W. (1969), "The Duration of the Egyptian Bondage," *Bibliotheca Sacra*, 126:306-316, October.

Hoehner, Harold W (1974), "Chronological Aspects of the Life of Christ–Part IV: The Day of Christ's Crucifixion," *Bibliotheca Sacra*, 131:241-264, July.

Holding, James Patrick (2001), "Copyist Errors," [On-line], URL: http://www.tektonics.org/copyisterrors.html.

Jackson, Wayne (1982), *Biblical Studies in the Light of Archaeology* (Montgomery, AL: Apologetics Press).

Jackson, Wayne (1989), "Questions and Answers," *Reason & Revelation*, 9:18-19, May.

Jackson, Wayne (1991), "The Holy Bible–Inspired of God," *Christian Courier*, 27:1-3, May.

Jacobus, Melancthon W. (1864), *Notes on Genesis* (Philadelphia, PA: Presbyterian Board of Publication).

Jamieson, Robert, et al. (1997), *Jamieson, Fausset, Brown Bible Commentary* (Electronic Database: Biblesoft).

Jevons, W. Stanley (1928), *Elementary Lessons in Logic* (London: MacMillan).

Josephus, Flavius (1987 reprint), *Antiquities of the Jews*, in *The Life and Works of Flavius Josephus*, transl. William Whiston (Peabody, MA: Hendrickson).

Kaiser, Walter C. Jr., Peter H. Davids, F.F. Bruce, and Manfred T. Brauch (1996), *Hard Sayings of the Bible* (Downers Grove, IL: InterVarsity Press).

Keil, C.F. and F. Delitzsch (1996), *Keil and Delitzsch Commentary on the Old Testament* (Electronic Database: Biblesoft), new updated edition.

Kenyon, Frederic (1939), *Our Bible and the Ancient Manuscripts* (London: Eyre and Spottiswoode).

Kitchen, Kenneth (1966), *Ancient Orient and Old Testament* (Chicago, IL: Inter-Varsity Press).

Kitchen, Kenneth (1980), *The Illustrated Bible Dictionary*, ed. J.D. Douglas (Wheaton, IL: Tyndale).

Lenski, R.C.H. (1961a), *The Interpretation of the Acts of the Apostles* (Minneapolis, MN: Augsburg).

Lenski, R.C.H. (1961b), *The Interpretation of the St. Luke's Gospel* (Minneapolis, MN: Augsburg).

Lenski, R.C.H. (1966), *The Interpretation of the Epistle to the Hebrews and of the Epistle of James* (Minneapolis, MN: Augsburg).

Leupold, Herbert C. (1942), *Exposition of Genesis* (Grand Rapids, MI: Baker).

Leupold, Herbert C. (1989 reprint), *Exposition of Daniel* (Grand Rapids, MI: Baker).

Lightfoot, John (1979 reprint), *A Commentary on the New Testament from the Talmud and Hebraica* (Grand Rapids, MI: Baker).

Lipscomb, David (no date), *Commentary on Second Corinthians and Galatians* (Nashville, TN: Gospel Advocate).

Lyons, Eric and Bert Thompson (2002), "In the 'Image and Likeness of God,' " *Reason & Revelation,* 22:17-32, March and April.

Mauro, Philip (no date), *The Wonders of Bible Chronology* (Swengel, PA: Reiner).

McCord, Hugo (1988), *McCord's New Testament Translation of the Everlasting Gospel* (Henderson, TN: Freed-Hardeman College).

McDowell, Josh (1975), *More Evidence that Demands a Verdict* (San Bernardino, CA: Campus Crusade for Christ).

McDowell, Josh (1999), *The New Evidence that Demands a Verdict* (Nashville, TN: Nelson).

McGarvey, J.W. (1875), *Commentary on Matthew and Mark* (Delight, AR: Gospel Light).

McGarvey, J.W. (1886), *Evidences of Christianity* (Cincinnati, OH: Standard).

McGarvey, J.W. (1892), *New Commentary on Acts of Apostles* (Delight, AR: Gospel Light).

McGarvey, J.W. (1902), *The Authorship of Deuteronomy* (Cincinnati, OH: Standard).

McKinsey, C. Dennis (1995), *The Encyclopedia of Biblical Errancy* (Amherst, NY: Prometheus).

McKinsey, C. Dennis (2000), *Biblical Errancy* (Amherst, NY: Prometheus).

Metzger, Bruce (1968), *The Text of the New Testament* (New York: Oxford University Press).

Miller, Glenn (1997), "Well, did Jesus Tell Them to Take a Staff or not? Another Contradiction?!" [On-line], URL: http://christian-thinktank.com/nostaff.html.

Morris, Henry M. (1976), *The Genesis Record* (Grand Rapids, MI: Baker).

Ozanne, C.G. (1970), *The First 7,000 Years* (New York: Exposition Press).

Paché, Rene (1971), *The Inspiration and Authority of Scripture* (Grand Rapids, MI: Eerdmans).

Pack, Frank (1975), *The Gospel According to John* (Austin, TX: Sweet).

Paine, Thomas (1795), *Age of Reason* (New York: Knickerbocker Press, 1924 reprint).

Pfeiffer, Charles F. (1966), *The Biblical World* (Grand Rapids, MI: Baker).

Pfeiffer, Charles F. (1979), *Baker's Bible Atlas* (Grand Rapids, MI: Baker).

Pierce, Larry (1999), "Cainan in Luke 3:36: Insight from Josephus," *CEN Technical Journal*, 13[2]:75-76.

Rendtorff, Rolf (1998), "What We Miss by Taking the Bible Apart," *Bible Review*, 14[1]:42-44, February.

Richards, Larry (1993), *735 Baffling Bible Questions Answered* (Grand Rapids, MI: Revell).

Roberts, J.W. (1977), *The Letter of James* (Austin, TX: Sweet).

Robertson, A.T. (1930), *Word Pictures in the New Testament* (Nashville, TN: Broadman).

Robertson, A.T. (1997), *Robertson's Word Pictures in the New Testament* (Electronic Database: Biblesoft).

Robinson, Edward (1993), "The Resurrection and Ascension of Our Lord," *Bibliotheca Sacra*, 150:9-34, January, first published in 1845.

Rohl, David M. (1995), *Pharaohs and Kings: A Biblical Quest* (New York: Crown).

Rimmer, Harry (1936), *The Harmony of Science & Scripture* (Grand Rapids, MI: Eerdmans, 1973 reprint).

Sarfati, Jonathan (no date), "How do You Explain the Difference between Luke 3:36 and Genesis 11:12?" [On-line], URL: http://www.answersingenesis.org/docs/3748.asp.

Sarfati, Jonathan D. (1998), "Cainan of Luke 3:36," *CEN Technical Journal*, 12[1]:39-40.

Schultz, Hermann (1898), *Old Testament Theology* (Edinburgh: T&T Clark), translated from the fourth edition by H.A. Patterson.

Sewell, E.G. and David Lipscomb (1921), *Questions Answered* (Nashville, TN: McQuiddy).

Spence, H.D.M., and Joseph S. Exell, eds. (1978), *The Pulpit Commentary, Volume 4: Ruth, I & II Samuel* (Grand Rapids, MI: Eerdmans).

Summers, Ray (1950), *Essentials of New Testament Greek* (Nashville, TN: Broadman).

Templeton, Charles (1996), *Farewell to God* (Ontario, Canada: McClelland and Stewart).

Thayer, Joseph (1979), *A Greek-English Lexicon of the New Testament* (Grand Rapids, MI: Zondervan).

Thiede, Carsten Peter and Matthew D'Ancona (1996), *Eyewitness to Jesus* (New York: Doubleday).

Thiele, Edwin R. (1951), *The Mysterious Numbers of the Hebrew Kings* (Chicago, IL: University of Chicago Press).

Thompson, Bert (2000), *Creation Compromises* (Montgomery, AL: Apologetics Press), second edition.

Thompson, Bert (2002), "Questions and Answers—A Matter of Time," *Reason & Revelation*, 22:41-48, May.

Thornton, R. (1887), *Commentary on the Old Testament—Historical Books* (London: Society for Promoting Christian Knowledge).

Tobin, Paul N. (2000), "Mythological Elements in the Story of Abraham and the Patriachal [sic] Narratives," *The Rejection of Pascal's Wager*, [On-line], URL: http://www.geocities.com/paulntobin/abraham.html.

Trench, Richard C. (1949), *Notes on the Miracles of Our Lord* (Grand Rapids: Baker).

Unger, Merrill (1954), *Archaeology and the Old Testament* (Grand Rapids, MI: Zondervan).

Van Eck, Stephen (1999), "The Pentateuch: Not Wholly Moses or Even Partially," *Skeptical Review*, 10:2-3,16, September/October.

Vincent, Marvin R. (1975), *Word Studies in the New Testament* (Grand Rapids, MI: Eerdmans).

Vine, W.E., Merrill Unger, and William White Jr. (1985), *Vine's Complete Expository Dictionary of Old and New Testament Words* (Nashville, TN: Thomas Nelson).

Wellhausen, Julius (1885), *Prolegomena to the History of Israel* (Edinburgh: Adam and Charles Black), translated by Black and Menzies.

Wells, Steve (2001), *Skeptic's Annotated Bible*, [On-line], URL: http://www.Skepticsannotatedbible.com.

Whitcomb, John C. and Henry M. Morris (1961), *The Genesis Flood* (Grand Rapids, MI: Baker).

Willis, John T. (1984), *Genesis* (Abilene, TX: ACU Press), originally published by Sweet Publishing Company of Austin, Texas.

Wilson, Robert Dick (1929), *A Scientific Investigation of the Old Testament* (New York: Harper Brothers).

Wiseman, D.J. (1974), *The New Bible Dictionary*, ed. J.D. Douglas (Grand Rapids, MI: Eerdmans).

Woods, Guy N. (1972), *A Commentary on the Epistle of James* (Nashville, TN: Gospel Advocate).

Wycliffe Bible Commentary (1985), Electronic Database: Biblesoft.

Younker, Randall W. (1997), "Late Bronze Age Camel Petroglyphs in the Wadi Nasib, Sinai," *Near East Archaeological Society Bulletin*, 42:47-54.

Younker, Randall W. (2000), "The Bible and Archaeology," *The Symposium on the Bible and Adventist Scholarship*, [On-line], URL: http://www.aiias.edu/ict/vol_26B/26Bcc_457-477.htm.

Zerr, E.M. (1954), *Bible Commentary* (Bowling Green, KY: Guardian of Truth).

Zuidhof, A. (1982), "King Solomon's Molten Sea and (π)," *Biblical Archaeologist*, 45:179-184.

SUBJECT INDEX

SCRIPTURE INDEX

NAME INDEX

A

Adams, A.W.–139
Africanus, Julius–162-163
Aikenhead, Thomas–7
Albright, William F.–44
Archer, Gleason–109,131-135,186,190
Aristotle–11
Arndt, William–137
Astruc, Jean–40

B

Barker, Dan–6,165,167,207
Barnes, Albert–101,136,138,151,190,210
Blomberg, Craig–200
Boles, H. Leo–90
Brauch, Manfred–82
Brown, Andrew–41
Bruce, F.F.–82,141
Burrows, Millar–57

C

Caesar, Julius–142
Cassuto, U.–27
Cheyne, T.K.–42,49

Clarke, Adam–71,122,149,200
Clayton, Peter–50
Clements, Tad–167

D

Davids, Peter–81
de Morgan, Jacques–43
DeHaan, M.R.–63
Delitzsch, Franz–25,47,69-70,108,137,149

F

Fairbairn, Patrick–163
Fee, Gordon–85
Finkelstein, Israel–45,49
Foster, R.C.–167
Free, Joseph–43,50,52

G

Gaussen, L.–7
Geisler, Norman–26,130,189
Godet, Frederic–158
Gottwald, Norman–41,49
Graf, Karl–40